DII73979

THE SCULPTURE OF PICASSO

FRONTISPIECE: *Glass of Absinth*. 1914. Painted bronze with silver spoon, 8½ inches high. The Museum of Modern Art, New York, gift of Mrs. Bertram Smith

ROLAND PENROSE

THE SCULPTURE OF
PICASSO

CHRONOLOGY BY ALICIA LEGG

THE MUSEUM OF MODERN ART, NEW YORK

IT DOES NOT SEEM TO PICASSO HIMSELF, he says, that the elements of his art have altered from period to period. Whatever means of expression his subject has called for, he has unhesitatingly adopted. His production is characterized on the one hand by maximum variability, on the other by unity and consistency. This has become apparent in exhibition after exhibition of his painting. But until the great retrospective *Hommage à Pablo Picasso* was organized in Paris to honor the artist in the 85th year of his life, there had been no comprehensive showing of Picasso's sculpture, for the simple reason that he had kept so much of it for his own enjoyment and took no interest in exhibiting it.

First and foremost, therefore, the Trustees of The Museum of Modern Art acknowledge their indebtedness to Picasso himself for his generous loans, most of which will be seen for the first time on this side of the Atlantic in the present exhibition. This is based essentially on the sculpture section of the Paris retrospective assembled by Jean Leymarie in 1966. Like the show of Picasso's sculpture sponsored by the Arts Council of Great Britain at the Tate Gallery in London in the summer of 1967, it has been directed by Sir Roland Penrose, who also wrote the penetrating interpretive essay for this publication.

Special thanks are due to André Malraux, Ministre d'Etat chargé des Affaires Culturelles, and to the Association Française d'Action Artistique for its sponsorship. We have also benefited throughout by the wholehearted cooperation of Gabriel White and, in particular, Joanna Drew of the Arts Council for assisting in innumerable details of organization and facilitating the photography of many of the works. We are especially grateful to all the museums and private collectors who have graciously participated in our undertaking and whose names are listed below.

No examination of Picasso is possible without reference to the years of study of his work by Alfred H. Barr, Jr., former Director of Collections at The Museum of Modern Art, culminating in his classic monograph *Picasso: Fifty Years of His Art*. Furthermore, it was to Mr. Barr in person that the artist granted his consent to lend us more than 200 objects from his own collection. The installation at the Museum was designed and executed by René d'Harnoncourt. Alicia Legg, Associate Curator of Painting and Sculpture, has assisted in the planning and execution of both exhibition and publication since their inception and has prepared the Chronology (pages 39-47). Many others of our staff, too numerous to mention, have contributed suggestions and by their combined efforts have made possible the realization of this project.

Monroe Wheeler
COUNSELLOR TO THE TRUSTEES
THE MUSEUM OF MODERN ART

LENDERS TO THE EXHIBITION

Larry Aldrich, New York; Mrs. Gilbert W. Chapman, New York; Mr. and Mrs. Alan H. Cummings, Winnetka, Illinois; Mr. and Mrs. Sampson R. Field, New York; Mr. and Mrs. Victor W. Ganz, New York; Mr. and Mrs. Gerald Gidwitz, Highland Park, Illinois; Joseph H. Hirshhorn Collection; Mr. and Mrs. Sylvan Lang, San Antonio, Texas; Lady Penrose, London; Pablo Picasso, Mougins, France; M. and Mme Georges Ramié, Vallauris, France; Sir Robert and Lady Sainsbury, London; Mrs. Bertram Smith, New York; Mrs. G. David Thompson, Pittsburgh;

The Baltimore Museum of Art; The Art Institute of Chicago; The Museum of Modern Art, New York;

Heinz Berggruen, Paris; Galerie Beyeler, Basel; Galerie Chalette, New York; Galerie Louise Leiris, Paris.

CONTENTS

IN ANY SPECULATION as to which of the visual arts first came into being in the infancy of man's consciousness, it would be possible to make strong claims for sculpture. That crucial advance in human development, the first use of tools, which must have happened about as early as the domestication of fire, gave man a greatly increased ability to do things for himself. But an even greater change in his destiny occurred when it dawned on him that the tool could also be used as a weapon and could add effectively to his powers of aggression and self-defense. The resulting prestige and emotional significance of a stone already sharp enough to cut wood rose to great heights when it became an instrument with the power of breaking skulls, the arbiter of life or death.

This is not the place to attempt to trace the transition that seems to have followed from the tool and the weapon to the work of art, but it is noticeable that certain characteristics remain common to both. The admirable precision of form of a chipped flint, adapted originally to the hand that held it and to the scraping or cutting it was required to do, gives us an aesthetic pleasure; and the implication of power contained in the club, the axe, or the knife blade may probably be considered to be analogous to the emotional power of a work of art.

I would suggest that the link is to be found in the process of diversion of aim, or ritualization, as described by ethologists in the behavior of animals. In a similar way the weapon, potentially an instrument of aggression and genocide, forfeits its original significance and yet retains the non-violent power we find in sculpture.

In the Cook Islands there are jade axe heads designed as tools and weapons, but they are fixed on elaborately carved stands so that it is impossible for their use to be either utilitarian or aggressive; instead they are revered ritualistically as objects of awe and admiration. They become symbols of a powerful bond of unity and love within the tribe.

Independent of this symbolization of power there is another tendency, the origins of which seem equally remote, which appears to have a strong influence on the emotional power of sculpture. Man has the desire to see in certain objects a likeness to himself or to some other object of importance, though it be of an entirely different nature, and to attribute to it, in consequence, a vicarious form of life. The accidental likeness of stones or clouds to the human head, or of mountains, rocks, or gorges to our anatomy, has without doubt had ominous significance for our ancestors and continues to have a baffling fascination for us. To this we may add the ancient and universal habit of finding association between male fertility and the phallic shapes of stones. Philosophers, psychiatrists, and art historians have had much to say on this account. Herbert Read tells us that "Some of Hegel's theories are worthy of Herodotus and in this spirit he (Hegel) suggests that the first monuments were phallic,"[1] but Read also makes it clear that these objects of veneration may vary in size from pebbles or amulets to giant standing stones or menhirs.

(Symbolism and metamorphosis are present in varying degrees in all sculpture, and they reach a high degree of significance in the work of Pablo Picasso.) These are qualities that are not so directly evident in painting, where illusion, more or less sophisticated, is at the basis of visual experience. (Sculpture has a fundamental advantage in that it appeals through the sense of touch as well as of sight, and because in its simplest state it requires no tools; only hands, to model its form.)

Another more fundamental analogy connects sculpture with life itself. The process of birth brings independent living organisms into the world, and it is in no way frivolous to compare this with the creation of sculpture in clay, bone, wood, or any other material that can be endowed with imaginary life. The biblical myth that Eve was made from a rib extracted from Adam during his sleep is remarkably close to the current theory that inspiration springs from the subconscious and is connected intimately with an obsession for a beloved person. Picasso's

assertion that each one of his works is a phial filled with his own blood has an archaic echo.

More than any other artist of our time Picasso has had the audacity to find his way back to the essentials of art by rediscovering its source. In sculpture, thanks to its basic primeval qualities, he is able to get even closer to the primitive emotional significance of art than in any of the other mediums, including painting, that he has used.

In the spring of 1933 Picasso produced a series of 46 etchings known as "The Sculptor's Studio," a theme not found in his work at any other time. This happened with a characteristic burst of energy, when, for the second time in his career, he was absorbed by an interest in sculpture. Some five years before, working with his old friend the Spanish sculptor Julio Gonzalez, he began to give new scope to his talent in this art. Gonzalez was an excellent craftsman in metal and with him Picasso explored new ways of constructing figures in this medium. The extraordinary inventions that were the result of his friend's assistance did not, however, occupy Picasso's entire activity for long; it was the production of greater than life-size heads and female figures modeled in plaster that began to overcrowd the stables at Boisgeloup. These sculptures showed more similarities to Picasso's own paintings of the time, in which the dominant theme was a nude, blonde and voluptuous, than to the cactus-like, wrought-iron sculptures made by his friend. It is these massive heads (pages 74-77) that appear among other sculptures in the etchings of 1933.

Using the sensitive line of the engraver, Picasso transposed the scene from twentieth-century Normandy to the mythical atmosphere of ancient Greece. The sculptor became a bearded Athenian, nude like the heroes and crowned with garlands. With him is his muse, sometimes posing for him but more often resting on a couch beside him, naked and beautiful, in contemplation of the work she has inspired. This shift in atmosphere does not happen without a touch of mockery aimed at academic classicism. Whenever Picasso introduces mythical characters into his work one can suspect that in reality he is making an important commentary on himself and his own problem because the characters never correspond exactly to their classical prototypes. They are in fact heroes or monsters of his own creation. These engravings can be thought of as delightful fantasy with no legendary significance, or seen as Picasso's thoughts and doubts about his own work, its effect on others, and its relationship to reality. A precarious situation arises in which he is caught by his love for his companion on the one hand, and on the other by the rival claims of his overriding passion for his art.

In the print dated March 21 (page 11), the sculptor and his model sit together. Her attention is fixed on a sculpture of her head, one of the great plaster heads finished a year before in the Boisgeloup workshop. The drawing leaves no doubt about the difference between her and her portrait. She is soft, warm, alive, and enquiring, whereas the sculpture is hard and immobile. We feel a contrast between the transitory life and ephemeral beauty of the model and the more lasting quality of a stone carving. But there is no rapt look of reverence for the work of the master in her eyes; instead there is a puzzled, contemplative scrutiny of this new intrusion into their lives. The reason for her doubt could be that the sculptor has not fallen into the time-honored trap of attempting to flatter his model by a lifelike but lifeless copy of her charms. Although there is a tantalizing resemblance in the profile, the bust demands our attention for other reasons: the exaggerated sweep of the line of nose and forehead, the solemn, monolithic elision, simple and convincing, uniting hair with cheek, and the outline of the eye, incised on the smooth surface. All these give it a personality, a presence of its own.

The etching conveys the inevitable contrast between the living model and the life with which the sculptor endeavors to animate his work. He already appears to be in a state of doubt and melancholy detachment. His interest has shifted and is now concentrated on things beyond the scope of his art—the fish swimming in a bowl that he holds in his hand. Movement, transparency, and the baffling fluidity of water are beyond his grasp.

In several engravings the Boisgeloup heads are examined critically in relation to the model, or rather reality. Sometimes they give a feeling of solidity, and at others they are transparent, like a diagram plotting in depth the planes and fundamental construction of the features. Also there is a plate in which a surrealist construction appears, closely resembling other projects for sculpture of this period where Picasso has invented anatomies composed of pumpkins, apples, tables, ladders, or sticks held precariously together (pages 14, 213).

There are other plates where the sculptor and his companion recline on cushions beside some incredible tour de force of his creation. The subjects are groups of figures in motion such as three youths performing acrobatic marvels, a bacchanalian dance by a garlanded youth, a bull, and a naked maiden (page 17), a bull goring two horses, and a centaur embracing a voluptuous nude. In fact, difficult subjects for any sculptor to choose to carve in the round, and certainly not subjects that Picasso would seriously attempt to realize himself. Throughout, however, the sculptor is captivated, amazed, and disquieted by his own invention.

To go further and examine another series of eleven engravings,[2] the product of concentrated work during the summer of 1933, the parallels with Picasso, his work, and his inner hopes and fears become even clearer. In early years Picasso found an analogy between himself

13

and Harlequin: the amorous, melancholy trickster, the outcast, the jester who lies in order to speak the truth. In many paintings Picasso even introduced him as a self-portrait. Harlequin continued to make his appearance in a more detached way in cubism and then disappeared. But in these eleven etchings another mythical character suddenly intrudes into the seclusion of the sculptor's studio. The lusty appearance of the Minotaur in his dual nature, half-man half-beast, seems immediately acceptable, even enjoyable, as a diversion and liberation from restraint. Surrounded by classical busts made by the sculptor, the Minotaur reclines amiably with the artist's model and respectfully raises his glass of wine to her placid beauty, or plays with her on a couch.

In the third engraving (page 22) the party is already well under way. The sculptor, liberated from doubt, has sunk into the cushions between two naked girls and exchanges greetings with his brutish but captivating companion. The orgy is followed by a moment of serenity. The monster is asleep behind a curtain, watched over like a child by an adoring woman (page 27). In the next plate, however, uncontrolled urges break loose—the Minotaur throws a woman from her horse and assaults her on the ground (page 28). In three etchings following, the scene changes abruptly. The divine beast, the intolerable monster, lies mortally wounded in the arena. The spectators look on in awe, while a woman stretches forward to touch the hump on the creature's awful back (page 31).

This sequence, which came to an end in June 1933, was given a postscript in the autumn of the following year. Picasso found another kind of penance for the monster—blindness. In four dramatic engravings he presents the horned demigod chastised, blinded, and feeling his way along the quay while the astonished fishermen watch from their boats. A little girl leads him by the hand. In the first engraving of this series (page 33) there is a detail that strengthens the view that the Minotaur had become Picasso's analogy for himself in the sculptor's role, just as formerly he had found an image of his own mercurial nature as a painter in Harlequin. This time, however, there is no insistence on any physical likeness. On the wall toward which the Minotaur is feeling his way hangs a picture of a violent scene suggesting David's painting of the death of Marat. It is placed upside down and crossed out deliberately by two sweeping lines. There is no means of knowing how far this is meant as a deliberate sign that painting has now lost its interest for the blind Minotaur, but it is clear that the insistence on his sense of touch implies that sculpture, which can be felt, still exists even though it cannot be seen. This is reminiscent of Picasso's early references to blindness during the blue period and the compensation for it that he suggests in paintings such as *The Blind Man's Meal* of 1903 and the etching *The*

Frugal Repast of 1904, where the hands of blind men bring them satisfaction by feeling and caressing an object or a loved companion. All this considered, it seems likely that it is not the ponderous laurel-crowned sculptor himself with whom Picasso wishes to associate himself but rather the Minotaur. His powerful, earth-bound, lusty nature, his spontaneous, instinctive behavior, outrageous and yet endearing, make this analogy more appropriate. Nor has he anything in common with his forerunner, Harlequin, except his amorous devotion to women and his reputation as a rogue and an outcast from society, a reputation that endeared both characters to Picasso.

I do not wish to suggest that there is any serious division between Picasso the sculptor and Picasso the painter. On the contrary, throughout the great diversity of his work it is noticeable how closely knit are all forms of expression and in particular the two major arts in question. It is impossible to consider one without the other. There are a great number of drawings and paintings that are virtually projects for sculpture (pages 211-214) and many in which the form is so emphasized as to appear solid. In addition, the cubist movement was primarily an enquiry into our perception of form. It was during this period that the first painted constructions appeared (pages 58-64), offering new solutions for problems of two-dimensional and three-dimensional techniques. The application of color to sculpture, again an ancient practice, is one that Picasso uses as a sculptor when he puts color into cubist constructions and as a painter when he paints human features on the flat surfaces of his sheet-iron sculptures. The result of his frequent reversal of techniques and his disrespect for conventions is rich in unexpected combinations. Finally both arts become fused completely in his treatment of ceramics.

In his youth Picasso proved his talent as both a sculptor and a painter by becoming highly skilled in conventional styles and mediums. His earliest known sculpture is a small bronze *Seated Woman,* 1901 (page 50), which he modeled when he was twenty. The attitude of the figure is similar to the crouching women who clutch to their breasts their half-starved children in his paintings of the blue period. It is as though painting had not satisfied his desire to know his model, to embrace her with all his senses. The simplifications of the folds of her dress and the melting of the limbs into the compact shape of her body show that the young painter already had the sensibility of a sculptor, an opinion that is confirmed by two small but extraordinarily expressive bronze heads modeled by him some three years later. In these Picasso showed at once his interest in facial expression, a passion that he has never lost and that in our century has been seriously on the decline among artists in general. The *Mask of a Blind Singer,* 1903 (page

51), is an example of his power to convey character and action with dramatic insight. The eye sockets are empty and dead in contrast to the open mouth and tense lips. A complete antithesis is to be found between this tortured face and the *Mask of a Picador with a Broken Nose*, 1903 (page 51), where the eyes with their distant stare and the firmly closed mouth carry a strong extrovert expression. Other heads such as those of *Fernande*, 1905-1906 (page 53), and *Alice Derain*, 1905 (page 53), are equally revealing as character studies, but in the *Head of a Jester*, 1905 (page 52), other considerations make their appearance.

Picasso has told how he modeled this head late at night after returning from the circus with Max Jacob. Although in the early stages the clay took the appearance of his friend, he continued to work on it until the only likeness to his model was in the lower part of the face. He had become more interested in the way a rough broken surface caught the light and in adding the crowning complement of a jester's cap. Other sculptures of this period were more experimental and have not survived.

In the summer of 1905 Picasso paid a short visit to Holland. Seen against the flatness of the landscape, the opulent forms of the Dutch girls inspired him to capture their massive charms in sculpture as well as in paint. The painting of a nude known as *La Belle Hollandaise* is a well-known example of his first attempts to convey the sculptural qualities of the human form in his paintings with subdued colors, as he did later in the colossal nudes of the early 1920s (page 212). With the exception of the bronze kneeling figure *Woman Combing Her Hair,* 1905-1906 (page 49), an example of Picasso's power to realize the massive, rounded strength of a nude with tenderness and charm, the sculptures that followed show a movement toward simplicity and stylization. In his first enthusiasm of 1905 he was tempted to make sculpture his major preoccupation. However, this did not happen.

During the revolution in his attitude toward painting that reached its crisis in the winter of 1906-1907 when he painted *Les Demoiselles d'Avignon* (page 211), two surprising new influences made themselves felt. Both came from sculpture hitherto unknown or unappreciated. He first became aware of the archaic vigor of pre-Roman Iberian sculpture (page 211), which had recently been found in excavations near his native town Málaga, and of a polychrome portrait bust of the same period, known as the *Lady of Elche,* which had been acquired by the Louvre in 1897. Their unorthodox proportions and their robust lack of refinement attracted Picasso, and these qualities soon made themselves felt in his own drawings and paintings and brought a new vitality into his work. This influence however soon became merged with another discovery that was to play an even greater role in the growth of his understanding of the significance of form. African sculpture had been discovered by his friends Vlaminck, Matisse, and Derain, who had begun to collect masks and wood carvings as early as 1904. Although they felt the attraction of the exotic associations and the emotive power of Negro art, they were unable to incorporate its significance into their own work. Picasso, to their consternation, combined both the influence of Iberian and African sculpture in his great painting *Les Demoiselles d'Avignon,* but it took him many years and devious excursions before he resolved the profound and subtle implications of these two influences in sculpture. Painting, however, served in some ways as a testing ground for sculpture. Already in 1908 he reduced his use of color almost to monochrome to allow the sculptural to assert itself unconfused.

There were, however, some direct results of African influence in three-dimensional work, particularly in the wood carvings, of which there is a splendid rough-hewn example dating from 1907 (page 55). For these he sometimes made working drawings with indications in color (page 211). The abrupt and radical changes of style through which he was passing tore him away from such direct influences and set him on a path that was to lead him to the discoveries of cubism.

Cubism can be described as a movement among painters toward the sculptor's three-dimensional problems. Its preoccupation with form and the desire to become conscious of an object from all sides, even entering into its inner structure in order to understand it, was opposed to former movements that had been concerned with impressions of color, atmosphere, and outline. In the tearing apart of the external appearance of objects, Picasso and Braque had set themselves the task of penetrating into reality and analyzing form into separate geometric components while presenting simultaneously several views of the same object, as though the spectator were walking round it or turning it over in his hands. The results were so convincing that for a while more ordinary ways in three-dimensional sculpture of arriving at a similar effect did not interest Picasso and never then or in later years held Braque's attention for long. Apart from three small isolated studies, one of a head and two of apples, modeled in 1910, the only examples of cubist sculpture in the round are the *Woman's Head* of 1909 (page 56) and the *Glass of Absinth* (frontispiece). Of the former we know something of Picasso's reactions. According to Gonzalez, Picasso said that in early cubist paintings "it would have sufficed to cut them up – the colors, after all, being no more than indications of differences in perspective, of planes inclined one way or the other – and then assemble them according to the indications given by the color, in order to be confronted with a 'sculpture'."[3] The cubist methods Picasso had begun to use in painting were in fact closely related to sculpture, and in the *Woman's Head,* on which he had set to work in Gonzalez' studio, he wished to apply them literally. He was determined to see how far he could revolutionize the perception of an object in three-dimensional technique.

Talking of this recently he said to me, "I thought that the curves you see on the surface should continue into the interior. I had the idea of doing them in wire." This solution, however, did not please him because, he added, "it was too intellectual, too much like painting." This indeed suggests that he was looking for more primitive qualities in sculpture and also that momentarily he was not inclined to pursue this analysis in depth any further. He decided on a compromise, in which the head retained its solidity and volume, while the surface was broken up into facets closely related to the analytical geometric planes he had used in cubist paintings inspired by the same model.

Having solved the problems presented by this particular piece, Picasso abandoned sculpture in the round almost entirely for about twenty years. However, during this time the far-reaching discoveries of cubism led him to a new form of union between the two arts. In November 1913 the poet Guillaume Apollinaire became editor of a monthly review, *Les Soirées de Paris,* and published four reproductions of cubist constructions made by Picasso. These met with fierce disapproval from the subscribers and proved nearly fatal to the review. The constructions were the logical development of the cubist collage, an invention that had saved cubism from becoming an esoteric abstract style by the introduction of scraps of newspaper, cigarette packages, or similar evidence of real objects among, and creating a contrast to, the illusions of painting. These constructions (pages 58-64), often brightly painted, broke the rules which demanded that a painting should remain two-dimensional and circumscribed by its frame; they came more into the category of the bas-relief, a compromise between two- and three-dimensional art. But this was not the only reason for the disapproval they aroused as outrageous innovations. The materials used by Picasso were of the most commonplace kind and therefore supposedly unworthy of a work of art. Any fragment of paper, wood, tin, cardboard, or string that suited his purpose was enlisted into this attack on former standards. The result was a composition in depth not contained within a frame, a revolutionary conception of new possibilities in both sculpture and painting.

Among the constructions there is, however, one small but notable three-dimensional polychrome sculpture, the *Glass of Absinth,* 1914 (frontispiece). It is still very close to those cubist still-life paintings and collages in which a wine glass appears (page 211), so dissected and recomposed that we are made conscious of its transparency, its roundness, and its essential hollowness as a container of liquids. The *Glass of Absinth* combines in a playful way varying degrees of reality. On top of the glass is placed a real absinth spoon holding a replica of a lump of sugar, but the glass is opened up in cubist fashion to show the surface of the liquid within. Each of the six bronze casts of the original wax sculpture was decorated differently by Picasso with a variety of textures or bright contrasts of lines and pointillist color. An opening in the side of the glass gave the appearance of transparency characteristic of all cubist constructions. The unbroken surface that received such respect and care in Picasso's early, more conventional sculpture had already begun to disintegrate in the *Woman's Head* of 1909; but cubism required a deeper penetration, which was to be carried further in the constructions. Here the object, usually a guitar or violin, was made to exist in depth by gaps and open spaces between its dismembered parts, giving simultaneously a sensation of transparency and solidity.

Unconcerned with their durability, Picasso chose to make the constructions in fragile materials, often using no more than pieces of cardboard painted and bent into shape, with strings stretched across from point to point. Unlike the *Glass of Absinth* and other constructions made in recent years they were not cast in bronze. The flimsy materials he used made this impossible. In consequence many of them exist no longer. It is therefore all the more surprising that they should have had such a rapid and widespread influence over sculptors who were looking for new methods of expression and new ways of extending the possibilities of their art. They are in fact the origin of the modern conception of sculpture that is built in space rather than modeled. One of the first indications of their influence is to be found in *Les Soirées de Paris* of June 1914, where Apollinaire published four reproductions of the latest works of Archipenko, two of which were polychrome constructions in wood, glass, and tin. About the same time (1914-1916) Vladimir Tatlin, who had met Picasso in Paris before returning to Russia, began to make his "corner reliefs," though his approach, unlike Picasso's, was purely abstract.

As a poet and the first interpreter of cubism, Apollinaire had realized the momentous importance of Picasso's use of sculptural volumes created in space. In his book *Le Poète Assassiné,* published in 1916, he tells a fantastic story of the monument designed in honor of the murdered poet by the artist he calls "l'Oiseau de Bénin" and who is meant to be Picasso. In the Bois de Meudon, l'Oiseau de Bénin chooses a site in a clearing where, discarding materials such as stone and bronze as "too old," he hollows out "a deep statue in nothing, like poetry and like glory." Then, having dug a life-size hole in the ground, he sculpts the interior in the likeness of Croniamantal, the poet, "so well that the void had the shape of Croniamantal, that the hole was filled with his phantom."[4]

Comparable with the constructions, but on a larger scale and equally transitory, were the giant figures of the "Managers" (page 212) designed by Picasso for Cocteau's ballet *Parade*. It was produced in Paris in 1917 by the Russian Ballet of Serge Diaghilev, and again Apollinaire showed his enthusiasm by writing in his introduction "that he saw in it the starting-point of a series of manifestations which should completely alter both arts and manners."[5]

Ignoring the revolutionary sculptural consequences of the cubist constructions, Picasso put all his energy into painting; and it was not until more than ten years later that he began to develop in three-dimensional sculpture the ideas launched so brilliantly in the constructions. However, his painting was never distant from sculpture. The massive nudes of the classical period of the early twenties (page 212) have much in common with the modeling of his early bronzes. Also there is a remarkable series of drawings made in 1924 (page 212), which were later published by Vollard to embellish his edition of Balzac's *Le Chef d'oeuvre inconnu*. They appear at first sight to be abstract doodles made up of lines with dots where they cross, like the knots in a net. But with Picasso art is never abstract, and if they are compared with the still-life paintings of the same period it becomes clear that they are variations on recurring themes. They are in general based on the shapes of musical instruments, particularly the guitar with its anthropomorphic associations; and like the cubist constructions they are a conception of transparent three-dimensional form. In this light the drawings become a logical step between the constructions and the next development in Picasso's sculpture, the iron and wire sculptures of 1928-1929. In these latter space has been enclosed by lines, and the three-dimensional form they draw in the air is based on a human figure surrounded by planes that create walls or

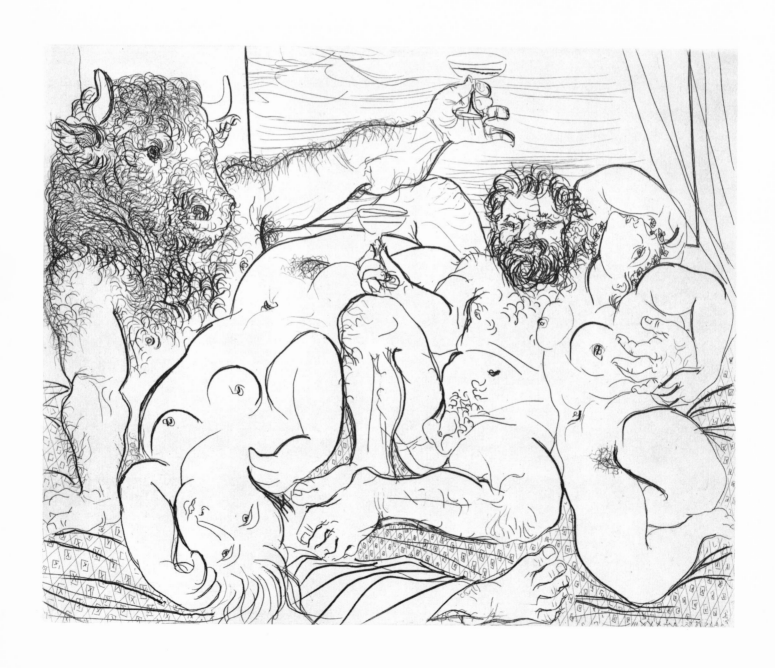

windows around it (page 65). A central transparent, ovoid form is enclosed by its transparent environment, giving an architectural homogeneity that it would be impossible to create in any other way. Together these works give us an idea of the close association between drawing and sculpture in Picasso's mind, in spite of their being some four years apart in date.

During this interval there is, in fact, a convincing example of the continuous dialogue between two- and three-dimensional means of expression. An almost identical resemblance occurs between a small painted metal construction of a circular head with a tripod as its base and the figure of the painter in a large canvas, the *Painter and His Model,* painted in the same year, 1928 (page 212).

But Picasso has not always wished to complete the dialogue. There are paintings and drawings of this same period that appear to be projects for sculpture (page 213). Their forms are so definitely modeled in light and shade that the transition could easily be made, but perhaps owing to his distaste for copying his own work this happened only indirectly. It is in his drawings, however, that there is the most convincing proof that he thinks and acts both as painter and sculptor. They have often been his means of exploring the subject he has had in mind and of deciding which medium was the one in which the final expression should take shape. This method has often served him well. At other times he has been guided by the material he has found or by the spontaneous development in which the material itself seems to work in collaboration with him.

Examples of the first process are the development of the cubist *Woman's Head* of 1909 (page 56), for which there exist several drawings (page 211), and the *Man with Sheep,* 1944 (pages 106-107). For this figure Picasso produced a great many drawings (page 214), large and small, before he decided which medium he should use. When finally it was clear to him that it should be a sculpture, modeled in the round, rather than a painting, the figure was completed with incredible speed.

The range of drawings for sculpture is also interesting in its great variety. Many drawings are given strong three-dimensional modeling using light and shade to obtain volume in the classical way. Some of these, dating as far back even as 1907, were never translated into sculpture but retained their three-dimensional qualities in paintings; whereas others were given solid form. When in later years Picasso became deeply impressed by Grünewald's Isenheim Crucifixion, he made from it drawings that amount to a sort of vocabulary of fantastic shapes, a process he carried further in the sheets of drawings made in 1933 of fantastic anatomies composed in the manner of Bracelli (page 213). None of these were translated literally into sculpture, although we often recognize the shapes reassembled in bronzes of later periods.

Perhaps the style that is both the simplest and the most demanding on the imagination is the line drawing in which the empty space contained by the line becomes mysteriously filled with form. This is true of representational line drawings such as we find in the etchings of "The Sculptor's Studio" and also of abstractions such as the cubist drawings and those astonishing statements of form in space used as decorations for *Le Chef d'oeuvre inconnu* (page 212) that are the forerunners of the space sculptures.

There are also working drawings such as the study for the Chicago Civic Center sculpture (page 214); closer still is the drawing of features on the flat surfaces of the sheet-iron sculptures themselves. There is in fact a unity of thought and of means that permits Picasso to employ his talent as a draftsman at any time throughout his work, whether it be purely graphic, or combined with collage, or three-dimensional sculpture.

All art to some degree implies a metamorphosis, a change of identity, at least in the material of which it is composed. The surrealists, with whom Picasso had become closely associated from the early twenties, saw in this an important challenge to conventional conceptions of reality and a fertile ground for the germination of poetic images. It is here that we find a close link between the theories of Breton and the developments in Picasso's sculpture that took place during the years between 1928 and 1935. This period for Picasso began with a small modeled sculpture, called *Metamorphosis,* 1928 (page 213), which coincides in date with a painting of the same title and subject. These works suggest a living organism with many attributes of the female form, but are composed in such a way that it would be wrong to describe them by such a definite title as "Woman." They are so compounded of what we know during our waking hours and what we recognize as a vision from our dreams that they escape categorical definition. By their ambiguous nature and convincing power, they acquire an independent reality. From this it can be implied that reality can never be satisfactorily stated except by paradox and that in Picasso's view the consciousness of contradiction and dialectical opposition is the guide to a new and clearer perception of truth. It is these tensions, he has stated firmly, that interest him rather than the search for a harmonious equilibrium. "I want to draw the spirit," he has said, "in a direction to which it is not accustomed and to awaken it."[6]

The great outburst of activity that had begun with the space constructions of 1928-1929 continued with metal sculptures composed of rough pieces of iron welded together. Fragments of machinery, kitchen utensils, and any piece of scrap that suited his purpose were incorporated. They were the most imposing sculptures he had yet realized. The biggest, the *Woman in the Garden,* 1929-1930 (page 67), is nearly seven feet tall. It incorporated its immediate environment in a more literal way than the space constructions, and the use of metal rods and sheet iron offered opportunities for new developments. In these works Picasso also began to exercise his genius for finding objects whose identity could be changed according to how and where they were placed in relation to the other parts of the sculpture. He obliged a metamorphosis to take place in individual parts as well as in the whole – a process that he has developed brilliantly in more recent years and that has since been widely used by sculptors in many parts of the world.

An example of the way in which Picasso mingles his theories and his work is his sudden return, shortly after making his wire drawings in space, to sculpture of a very different kind, more compressed in form than any he had ever attempted. In 1931, taking long narrow pieces of wood, he whittled out of them a series of slender figures that because of their proportions appear to have the stature of giantesses (pages 70-71). This ability to give scale to small objects so that they appear to be colossal is present throughout his work.

When Picasso makes a new discovery he does not continue to exploit it exclusively for long, nor did he at this time confine his energies to constructed sculptures. Remembering his early interest in the treatment of surfaces and the unifying virtue of the skin that encloses the body, he modeled in clay or plaster the group of monumental heads referred to earlier (pages 74-77). These began in 1931-1932 with the bust and bas-relief head of a girl, Marie-Thérèse Walter (pages 73-74). Starting from lifelike portraits he proceeded to treat her classical features with greater freedom, incorporating other influences, such as the exaggerated nose that might be ascribed to an imposing Baga mask which for years decorated the entrance hall of the château de Boisgeloup.

He relates that one night he built up a very complicated construction of wire, which looked incomprehensible until by chance his lamp projected the shadow on the wall. At once this looked to him like the profile of Marie-Thérèse. "I went on, added plaster and gave it its present form," he said, explaining: "When you work you don't know what is going to come out of it. It is not indecision, the fact is it changes while you are at work."[7]

Picasso during the Boisgeloup period was prolific, and there was great variety in his output. In addition to many new conceptions of the female form there are two important animal sculptures: the *Cock,* 1932 (page 83), and the *Heifer's Head,* 1932 (page 82). There is also a *Head of a Warrior,* 1933 (page 87), crowned with a crest like a Roman helmet, a sculpture in which Picasso has enjoyed aiming his humor at the popular conception of the hero.

A field that has given him great scope for treating conventional ideas with disrespect opened up when making dolls for his children, as he began to do during the thirties, and has continued at intervals since. The richest variety and the most surprising inventions come from his apt use of commonplace materials (pages 89-93). His desire to play, never entirely absent, is given full rein, and while he proceeds to bring a doll to life from the most unlikely scraps of waste he enjoys himself in the same way as the child for whom it is made. In this game the sophisticated research that went into cubism, the metamorphoses of surrealism, and the skill and cunning with which he can juggle with appearances all play their part with unimpeded spontaneity.

Paradoxically it was during the occupation of Paris, when materials were most difficult to obtain, that Picasso's production of sculpture reached a new intensity. The wartime sculpture was predominantly of the kind that relies on mass, texture, and surface tension, with metamorphic elements often playing an essential role. With the help of eager friends, many pieces were cast in bronze in spite of enemy restrictions. Casting gave unity to sculptures that were composed of heterogeneous elements, but to counterbalance the deadening effect this unification might produce, the bronze casts were given a new interpretation with paint.

In the great bronze *Man with Sheep,* 1944 (pages 106-107), however, Picasso chose to use simple and direct methods. More than a year before, he had begun to make studies of a bearded man holding a frightened sheep in his arms, and clearly because of this careful preparation he was finally able to achieve the modeling of the seven-foot figure in a day. On an already constructed metal armature he rapidly built up the figure with balls of clay, but not without moments of suspense when it seemed to Paul Eluard, who was present at the time, that the whole statue was about to collapse. The visual language he chose for this work was of immediate appeal. As though he wished at that time to make a communication easily understood by all, he deliberately took this archetypal theme to express himself in familiar terms. In doing so he sacrificed neither vigor nor tension. The surface treatment recalls the rough texture of the *Jester* of 1905 (page 52), but it has none of the melancholy softness of the blue period. The active play of light caught by the rugged epidermis, combined with the directional accents in the uneven texture, emphasize the man's rigidity in contrast to the confused struggles of the sheep.

The development in the link between the man and the sheep is interesting to follow. In the drawing of March 30, 1943 (page 214), the shepherd is the loving father who clasps a confident lamb to his bosom, but in the sculpture their relationship has changed fundamentally. There is no longer an ideal bond of love between them; this is replaced by a more realistic state of tension caused by necessity. The struggling animal no longer enjoys the protection of its master but submits to it perforce, putting to test the man's strength. The power of the relentless trap in which it is caught can be felt in the knotted sinews of the forearm and the firm grip of the hand. The man's reliance on his physical strength makes it obvious that in an ambivalent way the good shepherd is the shepherd who preserves his flock not for their immediate good but ultimately to be devoured by human society.

Another example of the eloquence with which Picasso can make the surface of his sculpture speak is found in the *Death's Head* (page 108), made in the same year. In this bronze the exterior has received an inverse treatment; instead of being given a rough surface to enliven it, it has been made smooth and covered with indentations like scars tearing into the dead,

polished covering of an empty vessel. This should be compared to the effect of fullness produced by another smooth surface, the tightly stretched skin of the breasts and belly of the *Pregnant Woman,* 1950 (page 125), in order to realize, among other things, the power with which Picasso can arouse two opposite reactions from the quality of smoothness. In the latter the effect was obtained simply by building three earthenware pitchers from a rubbish heap into the modeling of the body.

Although he often reminds us of his consummate skill in the more traditional techniques of sculpture, it is in his less conventional moods that Picasso provokes the most widespread reaction. His tactics, particularly his use of humor, affect us deeply and unexpectedly. In this field the wartime bronzes such as the *Woman with Apple,* 1943 (page 103), *"La Madame,"* 1943-1944 (page 102), and *Figure,* 1944 (page 99), are of great importance. They are highly complex in technique and are the heralds of a long series of sculptures that rely on modeling, impressions on the surface of borrowed textures, and the assemblage of objects. Sometimes

these things, picked up anywhere, are allowed to keep their identity, while at other times they are transformed and become something completely different.

The poetic value of ambiguity has become a factor of major importance in the art of this century. Picasso, who, to quote Paul Eluard, holds in his hands "the fragile key to the problem of reality"[8] has always been willing to probe our complacency about the identity of an object by showing that in certain circumstances it can mean something surprisingly different from the accepted interpretation. In consequence an equation such as "bicycle saddle plus handle-bars equals a bull's head" (page 109) has the disconcerting quality of a joke that contains serious implications. With the eye of a hawk and the cunning of an alchemist, Picasso assembled a series of important sculptures made from a rich variety of objects collected from beaches and rubbish dumps. Apart from their aesthetic values they induce a metaphysical enjoyment that is not far distant from the doubt and disquiet provoked by Hieronymus Bosch.

With the wealth he found daily in the rubbish around him in Vallauris, Picasso produced some memorable visual puns, such as the head of the *Baboon and Young, 1951* (page 134), made of two small automobiles found among his son Claude's toys. There are other smaller pieces, such as the little painted bronze *Woman Reading, 1952-1953* (page 135), which are made of rough pieces of wood, nails, and screws. They are astonishing for the grace and charm extracted from banal material. These metamorphoses are Picasso's way of doing the impossible things the legendary sculptor dreamed of as he gazed into his goldfish bowl, the making of which requires the powerful, seductive, and outrageous innocence of a Minotaur. In the *Goat Skull and Bottle, 1951-1952* (page 132), a composite sculpture unified by being cast in bronze and painted, the rays of light coming from the candle planted in the neck of the bottle are long, sharp carpenter's nails. The comparison between nails and penetrating light is a beautiful metaphor, a discovery that would be thought sufficient for one sculpture by most artists; but in this bronze smaller nails bristle between the horns of the dead animal with different meaning. They are a reminder of its former strength. In both cases the realm of sculptural expression is enriched. Another attack on the impossible is found in the *Little Girl Skipping Rope, 1950* (page 128). The limp rope itself becomes her support. The girl, her weight emphasized by the clumsiness of her boots, sails through the air above a hard metal flower. This concentrated sequence of absurdities gives exuberance and life to this emblem of nonsensical high spirits. There are other examples in which similar methods, which might have become restrictive or clumsy, result in tense and graceful sculptures such as the *Crane, 1952* (page 133), and the *Angry Owl, 1953* (page 135). The choice of materials in this last appears to be a deliberate expression of anger and aggressiveness. Pincers, screws, nails, and barbed metal fragments have served the artist well in the transformations he has brought about.

In spite of a continuous flow of new invention, Picasso did not abandon the discoveries he made in earlier years. Two large bronzes of flowers show how he could still give a new sense to a cubist technique. In the *Bunch of Flowers,* 1953 (page 137), he used the device of splitting open the closed form of the jar so as to appreciate it internally as well as externally, but with the flower, fragile and expansive by nature, he has taken the opposite line. He has made it solid, tightly packed like a bud ready to burst, and added delicate symbolic drawings of plants on the surface. In the other bronze, *Flowers in a Vase,* 1953 (page 136), it is the daring and irrational way of presenting flowers that is astonishing. To give that which is frail and ephemeral a solid and resistant appearance is the antithesis of all the principles of representational art. Picasso's blossoms are an enduring celebration of the triumph of flowers.

Since 1947 Picasso's activity as a sculptor has been accompanied by his work on ceramics (pages 120-123, 138-143, 196-197). According to Georges Ramié in whose pottery, la Madoura, in Vallauris Picasso has worked for nearly twenty years, "The rare and magnificent factor in his ceramics is his hands."[9] The manipulation of clay comes to him as naturally as does his skill as a draftsman. His supple, sensitive handling of the material produces forms that have the fullness of ripe fruit or the sinuous strength of a snake. Taking a pot fresh from the potter's wheel he kneads and twists it, and without losing the original fullness of its form a common vessel becomes the lithe body of a young woman or the fluttering shape of a brooding dove. "To make a dove," he has said, "you must first wring its neck."[10] Ceramics have given Picasso a wide field for experiment in which the element of chance, so frequently his ally, plays an important part. The boldness of his treatment has often alarmed his expert assistants, but they have had to admit, after almost every firing, that he can achieve effects impossible to all others.

Ceramics have the attraction for Picasso of combining painting and sculpture with utilitarian function. He has pursued each of these paths. There are tiles on which he has painted with boldness and sensitivity and a wide range of plates, vases, and pots. In his ceramic sculpture two of his most fundamental talents come equally into play: his ability to model clay in his hands and to draw rapidly with his brush on the surface. As a result he arrives at a complete fusion of sculpture and painting.

Picasso's love of modeling produced in 1945-1947 a series of small female figures that had in them the same primitive life that is to be found in the Catalan whistle figures, one of the oldest forms of popular art still existing in Mediterranean countries. Picasso's clay figures, now cast in bronze (pages 110-114), are a proof of his great respect for the most humble and yet most enduring traditions, which he combines with an unparalleled audacity of invention.

In a less distant way his most recent phase in sculpture can be traced to primitive origins. His painted sheet-iron sculptures are born from childhood games. When he was a boy he used to amuse his sister Lola by his dexterity with scissors and paper. He could make dolls, animals, and fantasies with magic speed. Running parallel with the immense variety that is character-istic of Picasso's work is the continuity with which throughout his life he has followed up his invention. He turned this talent—which for the amusement of friends can transform a wire from a champagne cork into a ballet dancer, and torn paper into creatures of fancy—to less ephemeral things. There are photos by Brassaï of some twenty folded-paper sculptures made in 1943 (page 214) that are all extraordinarily alive, but it was not until 1953 that he

found the means of enlarging and solidifying the small fragile maquettes by having them cut out and folded in sheet metal. In some cases the features of a face are painted on the surface; in others, drawn with arc welding. The result combines the two-dimensional significance of the drawing, the three-dimensional planes of the bent sheets, and the transparent space between the flat surfaces (pages 148-155, 169, 174-195, 198-206, 208). An illustration that stresses both the simplicity of Picasso's methods and the visionary foresight with which they are conceived is given by Lionel Prejger, who worked on their construction. He says that he was first presented by Picasso with a large sheet of brown paper on which a strange octopus-like shape had been drawn. "That is a chair," said Picasso, "and you see there an explanation of cubism! Imagine a chair that has been run over by a steam-roller, well, it would produce something like that."[11] Picasso then cut out the shape and folded the paper along lines he had already drawn, the final result being the *Chair, 1961* (page 175).

The sheet-iron sculptures are all carefully planned. With a delightful economy of means the simple sweeping curves of their outlines and the subtle play of light and shade on their surfaces combine to give them a sense both of movement and solidity. In many of them there is the clear-cut profile of Jacqueline, Madame Picasso; others are reminiscent of cubist constructions by the impression of transparency they establish. But whether they are birds, animals, or human figures they all possess the tensions and movement existing in life.

A further example of the continuity of Picasso's ideas is found in the attention he has given to the relationship between sculpture and architecture. It is already noticeable in drawings and paintings around 1930, which reveal him to be the potential architect and builder of fantastic sculptures large enough for people to live in. There is an important series of charcoal drawings of strange pregnant anatomies standing with monumental solidity against an empty horizon (page 213). He has said he had the idea originally that they should be built as monuments and placed along the Croisette, the seafront at Cannes. However, he changed his plan and, as he told D. H. Kahnweiler at the time, "I'll have to make paintings instead because nobody's ready to commission one from me."[12]

Recently, watching the rash of skyscraper hotels that sprout up around him along the coast, he has taken his imaginary projects further and filled large sketch books with drawings for buildings twenty stories or more high, like colossal sculptures on stilts. On their curved surfaces are balconies. The sweep of terraces and low domes gives (since Picasso's fundamental approach to everything is anthropomorphic) a sensation of organic life. "Why shouldn't you use curved surfaces for walls?" he said to me in conversation. "I would like to make houses from inside—like a human body, not just walls with no thought of what they enclose."

In the last few years the means of realizing some of his dreams of monumental sculpture has presented itself. Immense sandblasted concrete sculptures have been constructed by Carl Nesjar from Picasso's maquettes, made originally of tin or cardboard. The enlargement has always called for careful consideration using intermediary stages, as in the case of the *Woman with Outstretched Arms,* 1961 (pages 192-193).

The most important of his gigantic sculptures so far achieved is the great head in sheet steel some 60 feet high that is now being erected in the center of Chicago. In 1964 Picasso conceived this sculpture in response to an invitation to design a monument for the new Civic Center in that city. He had been well supplied with information about the site, and he produced a model in iron about four feet high (page 207), which he insisted was to be enlarged precisely to the size required by the architects and engineers. No doubt the result will be very

close to his original conception, a noble and severe monument made up of solid forms and the void. The conception of a sculpture built in steel, composed of the profiles and surfaces of sheet metal, with open spaces contained in the gaps between them and areas enclosed by iron rods, is connected with discoveries made fifty years earlier. Its sources are in the cubist constructions of 1912-1914 (pages 58-64). The iron rods in the Chicago monument have affinities with the guitars of the cubist constructions, and the transference of the idea of a musical instrument to the head of a woman gives poetic echoes. The conception belongs to the "drawings" in space of the wire sculpture of 1928-1929 (page 65) and the composite iron sculptures such as the *Woman in the Garden* of 1929-1930 (page 67). However, it is unlike any of its predecessors. Even among recent work there is only the small *Head of a Woman,* 1962 (page 206), which has some of the same features, less convincingly resolved. In this way Picasso's dream of a great monument, which he expressed in charcoal drawings and paintings more than thirty years before, has been realized.

It is difficult to find an explanation for the considerable difference in attitude that Picasso has towards his sculpture and his painting. Since his youth he has regarded painting as the most obvious and legitimate of his resources, and with certain important exceptions he has always been willing to part with paintings. Sculpture has had for him a more personal attachment: he has always wished to live surrounded by it, and only since his eighty-fifth birthday (1966) has he allowed a full-scale retrospective of his sculpture to be shown, first in Paris and later in London and New York. In his preface to the catalogue of the Picasso seventy-fifth anniversary exhibition at The Museum of Modern Art in New York in 1957, Alfred H. Barr, Jr., regretted that it had not been possible to show more than a few of the important sculptures, saying: "Had the many major pieces still in Picasso's possession been available (as was expected), the artist would, I believe, have been revealed as one of the great sculptors of our time." It is now possible to form an opinion of the significance of this art in his life and to estimate his influence on the development of sculpture throughout the world in this century.

It is possible to divide his work roughly into five major categories: the early modeled sculptures, which rely on volume and surface tensions; the cubist bas-relief constructions, based on indications of the shape of objects in space and built up into a transparent conception of form; then, after a period of some years, the wrought-iron constructions and modeled plasters of the late twenties and early thirties; the sculpture of the war and postwar years, with its emphasis on the use of found objects, combined with plaster and cast in bronze; and finally the sheet-iron and monumental sculptures with which he is still occupied. An important accompaniment during the last twenty years is his ceramics, in which the most primitive and fundamental motive for sculpture persists: the desire to mold clay in the hand. This immense panorama of his diverse styles in sculpture has now been assembled as the protean work of one man, and it will make clear to all that this aspect of his work can be considered a major element in his vast production. The current exhibition has at last given the opportunity to acclaim Pablo Picasso as a great sculptor and yet another reason to admire and wonder at the contribution he has made to our vision and our understanding of reality.

This essay is illustrated with four etchings from the series "The Sculptor's Studio," four from "The Minotaur," and one from "The Blind Minotaur." References are given on page 227.

Footnotes

1 Herbert Read, *The Art of Sculpture* ("Bollingen Series" 35:3, New York: Pantheon Books, 1956), p. 6

2 Milton S. Fox, ed., *Picasso for Vollard,* introduction by Hans Bolliger (New York: Harry N. Abrams, 1956), nos. 83-93

3 Julio Gonzalez, "Picasso Sculpteur," *Cahiers d'Art,* vol. 11, no. 6/7, 1936, p. 189

4 Guillaume Apollinaire, *Le Poète Assassiné* (Paris: L'Edition Bibliothèque des Curieux, 1916)

5 Roland Penrose, *Picasso: His Life and Work* (London: Victor Gollancz, 1958), p. 200

6 André Breton, "L'Ecart absolu générique," *L'Oeil,* no. 131, Nov. 1965, p. 36

7 Penrose, *op. cit.,* p. 244

8 Paul Eluard, *A Pablo Picasso* (Geneva, Paris: Trois Collines, 1947), p. 38

9 S. and G. Ramié, *Hommage à Picasso,* Petit Palais, Paris, 1966, n.p. (introduction to ceramics section)

10 Penrose, *op. cit.,* p. 325

11 Lionel Prejger, "Picasso découpe le fer," *L'Oeil,* no. 82, Oct. 1961, p. 29

12 D. H. Kahnweiler, *The Sculpture of Picasso* (London: Rodney Phillips, 1949)

Rogi-André: *Pablo Picasso*, 1935. Collection of The Museum of Modern Art

Concerned specifically with Picasso's sculpture, the following outline summarizes only briefly other aspects of his career, and omits some events of his life not related to this part of his work. The most recent general chronology of Picasso is contained in the catalogue of the exhibition Hommage à Pablo Picasso, *held in Paris during the winter of 1966-1967. A chronological listing of exhibitions that include sculpture and ceramics is contained in the bibliography (pages 215-220).*

1881

October 25: born Pablo Ruiz Picasso at Málaga (Andalusia), Spain, to José Ruiz Blasco, a painter and teacher at the San Telmo School of Arts and Trades, and Maria Picasso Lopez.

1891

His father accepts position of art master at the Instituto da Guarda, a secondary school in Coruña. The family settles in an apartment close to the school. Pablo works in his father's classes and soon masters the academic techniques of drawing from casts, and painting; he even finishes details in his father's still lifes. Discouraged by his own artistic achievement, Don José recognizes his son's talent and hands over to him his paints and brushes.

1895

The School of Fine Arts (La Lonja) in Barcelona offers his father a post as professor, and the family stops off in Madrid, where Pablo visits the Prado for the first time. Through his father's position at the school he is allowed to take the entrance examination for the advanced class in drawing, which he passes brilliantly.

1897

The academic interests of his father and family friends and the school curriculum provide insufficient intellectual stimulus to the young artist; he leaves for Madrid in October and is accepted in the advanced class at the Royal Academy of San Fernando, which he attends sporadically, not finding it any more challenging than the school in Barcelona.

1898-1899

Contracts scarlet fever and returns to Barcelona. Convalesces at Horta de Ebro (now called Horta de San Juan). Back in Barcelona, he joins the group of bohemian artists and poets at the café Els Quatre Gats ("The Four Cats"), among whom are Santiago Rusiñol, Miguel Utrillo, Ramón Casas, and Isidro Nonell, and the younger men Ramón Pichot, Sebastian Junyer-Vidal, Ricardo Canals, and Jaime Sabartés (who in later years becomes Picasso's secretary). These Catalan intellectuals interest him in the *fin de siècle* style of such artists as Toulouse-Lautrec, and attract him to other ideas and achievements in the arts of France and northern Europe. He also gains an appreciation of the Spanish masters El Greco, Velázquez, and Zurbarán, and of medieval Catalan art.

1900

First drawings published in the magazines *Joventut* and *Pèl & Ploma*. From October to December makes first visit to Paris. The dealer Berthe Weill buys three paintings.

1901

In Madrid briefly as art editor and illustrator of *Arte Joven*, a journal of which only two numbers appear. Returns to Paris in the spring. Has first exhibition at Ambroise Vollard's gallery. His paintings, reflecting his own limited funds and the life of the streets and cafés of Barcelona and Paris, have a pervasive melancholy, accentuated by cool, often blue tonalities, giving rise to the term blue period. The poet Max Jacob comes to the opening and seeks him out. Begins signing himself "Picasso," his mother's family name. First attempt at modeling: small bronze *Seated Woman* (page 50). Two small sculptures that soon follow, the *Mask of a Blind Singer* and the *Mask of a Picador with a Broken Nose* (page 51), are also related in mood to blue-period paintings.

1904-1905

Decides to remain permanently in France, and in the spring moves into a studio in a dilapidated tenement called the Bateau Lavoir, 13, rue de Ravignan (now Place Emile-Goudeau), which he occupies until 1909. Kees van Dongen and André Salmon are already there, and Max Jacob brings many other writers and poets, including Maurice Raynal and Guillaume

Apollinaire; it becomes known as the *rendezvous des poètes*. Among the artists Picasso sees about this time are the Spanish painters Canals, Pichot, and Juan Gris; the Spanish sculptors Manolo Hugué, Pablo Gargallo, and Julio Gonzalez; and, soon after, the French artists Derain, Léger, Rousseau, Matisse, and Vlaminck. Fernande Olivier, a fellow tenant in the building, becomes his mistress.

1905

Attracted to the life of the circus, he paints acrobats and clowns, his palette changing to warm tones, leading to the term rose period. Vollard casts a series of bronzes, among them the *Head of a Jester* (page 52). Work begins to interest American collectors Leo and Gertrude Stein and the Russian Shchukine. At the Salon d'Automne takes place the first showing of the fauves, a revolutionary group centering around Matisse; a special gallery of ten paintings by Cézanne especially impresses Picasso.

1906

Becomes acquainted with pre-Roman Iberian sculpture at the Louvre, some of which had recently been excavated; his paintings reflect their robust proportions and archaic features.

1907

African Negro sculpture had already been collected by Vlaminck, Derain, and Matisse, but Picasso makes his own discovery at the galleries of historic sculpture in the Trocadéro. Numerous studies made during the previous year now culminate in the painting *Les Demoiselles d'Avignon* (page 211). Several carved wood figures show the same African influence (page 55). Meets D. H. Kahnweiler, who has opened a new gallery, and Georges Braque.

1908-1909

Begins close association with Braque. Together they develop the style that becomes known as cubism. Models small *Seated Woman* (page 57).

1909

Woman's Head (page 56), a portrait of Fernande closely related to his drawings and paintings in the analytical cubist style (page 211), is modeled in the studio of Julio Gonzalez. Moves to a larger studio at 11, Boulevard de Clichy.

1911-1912

Painting style gradually alters from the shaded, faceted planes of analytical cubism to the use of flat color areas and pasted paper collage. In these works, references to his new mistress, Eva (Marcelle Humbert), appear, often in the form "Ma Jolie."

1912-1914

Principles of collage cubism applied to three-dimensional constructions of painted wood, cardboard, paper, string, and other commonplace and often ephemeral materials (pages 58-63).

1914

Models *Glass of Absinth* (frontispiece) in wax and makes six casts in bronze, each painted differently and incorporating a real spoon. Except for occasional experiments with construction, he then virtually abandons sculpture until 1928.

1914-1918

With the outbreak of war, Picasso is separated from many of his friends. Braque and Derain serve in the army. Apollinaire is badly wounded, and dies in the influenza epidemic of 1918. In 1915, Eva dies.

1917

Among other projects for the theater, with which he becomes deeply involved at this time, he designs the decor for Cocteau's ballet *Parade,* produced by Diaghilev's Ballets Russes; his costumes for the Managers represent cubist constructions on a monumental scale (page 212).

1918

Marries the dancer Olga Koklova. Takes an apartment at 23, rue la Boëtie, and works there.

1920-1927

During the twenties, Picasso's production in painting is extremely varied. Almost simultaneously he devotes himself to ponderous neo-classic figure compositions (page 212), and to synthetic cubist works such as the two versions of the *Three Musicians,* 1921, and the *Three Dancers,* 1925. In 1924 he does numerous ink drawings (page 212) whose networks of lines become transparent violins and guitars, reminiscent of the cubist constructions and anticipating later wire sculpture. Associates with André Breton and the Surrealists and participates in the first Surrealist exhibition at the Galerie Pierre in 1925.

1927-1928

During most summers Picasso has spent holidays in the South, first in Spain, later in southern

France, and often at the seaside. In the summer of 1927, at Cannes, he uses surrealist distortion in strongly modeled drawings of bathers, conceived as designs for monumental sculptures to be erected along the promenade La Croisette (page 156). The following winter he carries out this idea in sculpture with a small metamorphic figure in plaster (page 213), and in the summer, at Dinard in Normandy, makes further drawings on this theme.

1928-1931

In Paris, in 1928, Picasso enlists the aid of Gonzalez in welding metal, and produces iron-wire space constructions (page 65) and the painted metal *Head* (page 69). These sculptures closely parallel the paintings he is working on (page 212). Other important assembled metal sculpture that results from the collaboration with Gonzalez includes the large *Woman in the Garden* (page 67), and *Head of a Woman* (page 68). Several large paintings of 1929, representing bathers with skeletal forms and now called "bone" pictures, carry on the sculptural theme. In August 1930 at Juan-les-Pins he begins a series of relief constructions of various materials covered with sand (page 72).

1931

Through the years, along with major projects, he turns to manual crafts, transforming lengths of twisted wire into human form and, in 1931, whittling small elongated figures out of frame molding (pages 70-71).

1932

Although he retains his apartment in Paris, he buys a small eighteenth-century château in Boisgeloup, a village near Gisors (Eure). He transforms the stables into studios of various kinds, and the coach houses into sculpture studios. Here he produces a series of over-life-size heads in clay and wet plaster (pages 74-77) of his new model Marie-Thérèse Walter, of whom he also does many paintings, and who becomes his mistress. June 16–July 30: retrospective exhibition at Galeries Georges Petit, in which seven pieces of sculpture (including those on pages 67-68) are shown. A wide variety of work follows, including further modeled pieces in clay and plaster, and relief constructions.

1933

In February does a group of drawings called *An Anatomy*—more studies for fantastic sculpture "bathers" (page 213). From March to May he produces 40 etchings on the theme "The Sculptor's Studio," finishing the series the following year with six more.

1935
Separates from Olga, after several years of estrangement. Ceases to work at Boisgeloup.

1936
Outbreak of the Spanish Civil War. Meets Dora Maar, who later becomes his mistress.

1937
Takes a new studio at 7, rue des Grands-Augustins to work on a mural commissioned for the Spanish Pavilion at the Paris World's Fair. *Guernica* begun May 1 and completed early in June. Two of the colossal plaster sculptures executed at Boisegeloup, one a head (page 75), and the other a nude, are placed outside the pavilion, the first time such work is seen publicly.

1939
Picasso is in Antibes when war is declared in September. He spends part of next year in Royan, near Bordeaux, returning frequently to Paris.

1940-1945
Remains in Paris during the German occupation. Paints and again takes up sculpture at 7, rue des Grands-Augustins, living in rooms adjoining the studio. With the help of friends, who take plasters to a foundry at night in handcarts, he casts a large number of bronzes, including earlier work done at Boisgeloup. The finished bronzes are brought back the same way at great risk of being confiscated by German patrols. His hands never idle, he creates whimsical objects out of the most unexpected materials, by simply adding a feather to a piece of scrap metal, sticking a paper flower into a crust of bread, or embellishing pebbles with carving and paint. Paper is torn to make masks, figures, and animals, which he will later develop in metal. Many of these inventions remain only in the photographs of Brassaï (page 214) and Dora Maar.

1942
Begins a series of sketches of a bearded shepherd holding a sheep (page 214), which he plans to develop into a life-size sculpture.

1943
Meets Françoise Gilot, a young art student. Creates assembled sculptures incorporating actual objects, and impressing textures into plaster or clay (pages 98, 100-105, 109).

1944
Models *Man with Sheep* (pages 106-107) and *Death's Head* (page 108). In October, as a

tribute to his moral support of the Resistance, he is invited to show recent works at the Salon d'Automne; five sculptures are included (pages 75, 83, 97, 108-109).

1945

Models small figures in clay, continuing the series in 1947 (pages 110-113). Takes up lithography at the workshop of Fernand Mourlot. Françoise, by now his mistress, models for him.

1946

In spring goes to Antibes with Françoise. Director of the Antibes Museum, which occupies the Grimaldi Palace, offers him space and materials to paint. He leaves on permanent loan the paintings, drawings, etc. done there. Cement casts of two of the female heads of 1932 (pages 75, 77) have been added to the collection, now called the Musée Picasso.

1947-1948

In August 1947, revisiting the Madoura pottery of the ceramists Georges and Suzanne Ramié at Vallauris, near Antibes, he is delighted to see that the small figures he had casually modeled there the year before have been fired. This begins an intense interest in ceramics, which occupies him for more than a year. In 1948 he settles in the small villa La Galloise, later taking over an abandoned perfume factory for painting, sculpture, and graphics studios. In November 1948 a large ceramics exhibition is held at La Maison de la Pensée Française, Paris. Picasso has continued an enormous production in ceramics, including both sculpture (pages 120-123, 138-143, 196-197) and decorated bowls, plates, tiles, and urns of infinite variety.

1949

Buchholz Gallery, New York, shows 58 works, including the small bronzes of 1945 and 1947. This is the first of many Picasso exhibitions arranged by Curt Valentin.

1950

Continuing his work in ceramics, he also produces many modeled works to be cast in bronze, again using the found objects that over the years have distinguished his plastic art. Among these are such important works as the *Pregnant Woman* (page 125), the *She-Goat* (page 126) and the *Woman with Baby Carriage* (page 129) and *Little Girl Skipping Rope* (page 128). La Maison de la Pensée Française holds an exhibition of 43 sculptures dating from 1932 to 1943, and drawings of the forties.

Cast of *Man with Sheep* is erected in Vallauris, and Picasso is made an honorary citizen.

1953

Retrospective exhibitions in Lyon, Rome, and Milan, in which sculpture is importantly represented. Using wooden boards and fragments of molding, he assembles and paints human figures (pages 146-147) reminiscent of dolls and and other constructed figures of 1935 (pages 89-93) but on a larger scale. Françoise Gilot leaves Picasso.

1954

In April and May paints a series of portraits of a young girl, Sylvette David, and about the same time begins to work in sheet metal—cut, bent, and painted to create a series of busts and heads of Sylvette and of Jacqueline Roque, his new companion (pages 148-155).

1955

His estranged wife Olga dies. Moves to the large villa La Californie in the hills above Cannes. Retrospective exhibition in Munich, also shown at Cologne and Hamburg.

1956

Again builds figure constructions of scrap lumber, some of which he casts in bronze, such as *The Bathers* (page 156). Occasionally returns to this technique in later years, up to 1960 (pages 157-158, 160-161, 164-165).

1957

Seventy-fifth anniversary exhibition at The Museum of Modern Art, New York, including 42 bronzes of all periods. Subsequently shown in Chicago, and then in Philadelphia, where 75 ceramics, previously shown in London and Rotterdam, are added. This is the largest showing in America to date of his sculptural works.

1958

In March an exhibition of ceramics is held at La Maison de la Pensée Française. Paints a large mural for the new UNESCO building in Paris.

1959

A bronze cast of the 1941 *Head of Dora Maar,* donated by Picasso, is inaugurated as a monument to the memory of Guillaume Apollinaire in a square near Saint-Germain-des-Prés.

1960-1963

In November 1960 begins collaboration with Lionel Prejger in making large-scale sheet-metal sculpture, some, such as *Woman with Outstretched Arms,* over life size (page 193). With scissors, Picasso cuts the model directly out of paper or cardboard, then folds it to determine the form, marking the folds for the artisans who will cut the metal sheets. A remarkable three-dimensionality is achieved.

1961

Marries Jacqueline, March 13, and in June moves to present home, a large house called Mas Notre-Dame-de-Vie in Mougins, near Cannes.

1962

Renewing his interest in monumental sculpture, collaborates with Norwegian artist Carl Nesjar, who has developed a method of casting and sandblasting concrete (page 214). In April and May a large benefit exhibition, *Picasso: An American Tribute,* is held in nine New York galleries; includes a sculpture section at the Otto Gerson Gallery, containing 35 works from 1901 to 1960.

1965

Invited by the architectural firm Skidmore, Owings and Merrill to design a monument for the new Civic Center in Chicago. Completes a model in welded steel, 41 inches high (page 207), which is to be developed into a 60-foot-high sculpture by architects and engineers.

1966

From November 18, 1966, to February 12, 1967, *Hommage à Pablo Picasso,* eighty-fifth anniversary exhibition is held in Paris. Includes 284 paintings at Grand Palais; 205 drawings, 187 sculptures, and 116 ceramics at the Petit Palais; and graphic works at the Bibliothèque Nationale.

1967

From June 9 to August 13, the sculpture, ceramics, and several drawings from the Paris exhibition, principally from Picasso's own collection, are shown at the Tate Gallery, London. They also form the major part of the exhibition at The Museum of Modern Art, New York, from October 11, 1967, to January 1, 1968.

Kneeling Woman Combing Her Hair. 1905-1906. Bronze, 16⅜ inches high. The Baltimore Museum of Art, Cone Collection

ABOVE: *Mask of a Picador with a Broken Nose*. 1903? Bronze,
7¼ inches high
BELOW: *Mask of a Blind Singer*. 1903. Bronze, 5⅛ inches high
OPPOSITE: *Seated Woman*. 1901. Bronze, 5½ inches high

Head of a Jester. 1905. Bronze, 15 inches high.
Collection Mrs. Bertram Smith, New York

OPPOSITE.
ABOVE: *Fernande.* 1905-1906. Bronze, 13⅜ inches high

BELOW: *Alice Derain.* 1905. Bronze, 10⅝ inches high

52

LEFT: *Head of a Woman.* 1906. Bronze relief, 4⅞ x 2¼ inches.
Joseph H. Hirshhorn Collection

RIGHT: *Mask of a Woman.* 1908. Bronze, 7½ inches high.
Collection Mr. and Mrs. Sampson R. Field, New York

OPPOSITE.
ABOVE: *Figurine.* 1907. Bronze, after carved wood, 8⅝ inches high

BELOW: *Figure.* 1907. Wood, 32¼ inches high

54

56

BELOW: *Seated Woman.* 1908. Bronze, 4 inches high. Collection Mr. and Mrs. Alan H. Cummings, Winnetka, Illinois
OPPOSITE: *Woman's Head.* 1909. Bronze, 16¼ inches high. The Museum of Modern Art

58

Violin. 1913. Pasted paper, chalk and gouache on cardboard, 20 x 11¾ inches

OPPOSITE.
LEFT: *Guitar.* 1912. Sheet metal and wire, 30¾ inches high
RIGHT: *Violin.* 1913-1914. Cardboard and string, 23 inches high

ABOVE: *Glass, Pipe, and Playing Card*. 1914. Painted wood and metal, 13⅜ inches diameter
OPPOSITE: *Guitar*. 1914. Painted metal, 37⅜ inches high

Still Life. 1914. Painted wood with upholstery fringe, 18⅞ inches long. Collection Lady Penrose, London

LEFT: *Musical Instruments.* 1914. Painted wood, 23⅝ inches high

BELOW, LEFT: *Glass and Dice.* 1914. Painted wood, 9¼ inches high

BELOW, RIGHT: *Violin and Bottle on a Table.* 1915-1916. Painted wood, tacks, and string, 18½ inches high

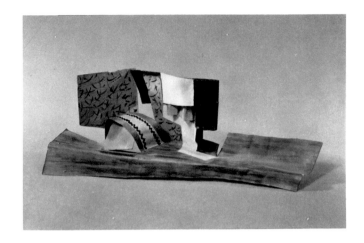

Packet of Tobacco. 1921. Painted metal, 18⅞ inches long

BELOW: *Guitar.* 1924. Painted metal, 42½ inches high

OPPOSITE: *Construction in Wire.* 1928-1929. 19⅝ inches high

Woman. 1930-1932. Iron, 31⅞ inches high

OPPOSITE: *Woman in the Garden.* 1929-1930. Bronze, after welded iron, 82¾ inches high

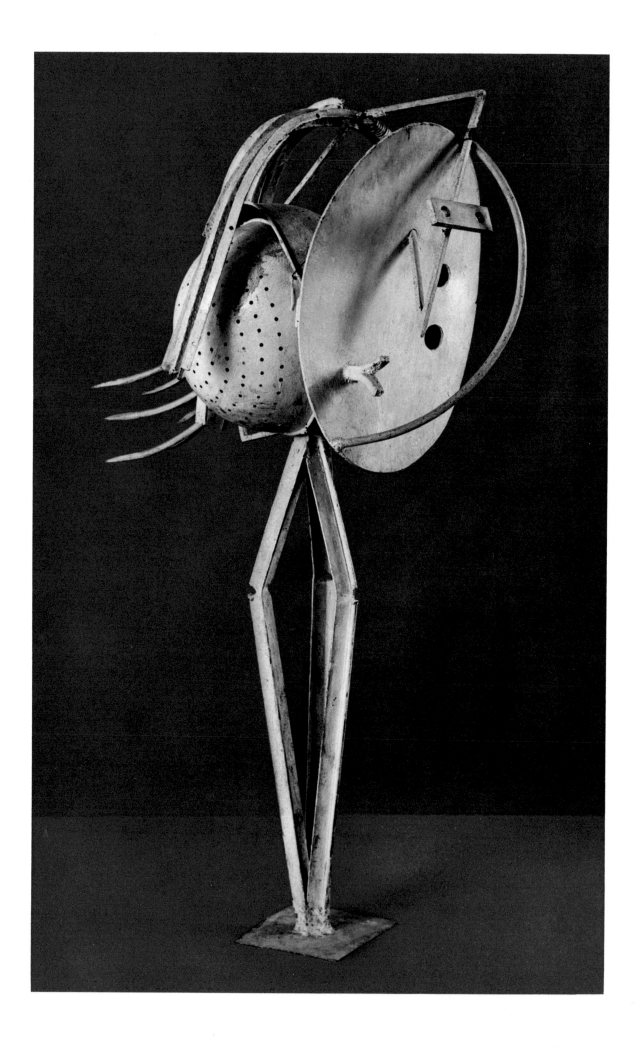

Head. 1931. Bronze, after welded iron, 33 inches high
OPPOSITE: *Head of a Woman*. 1931. Painted iron, 39⅜ inches high

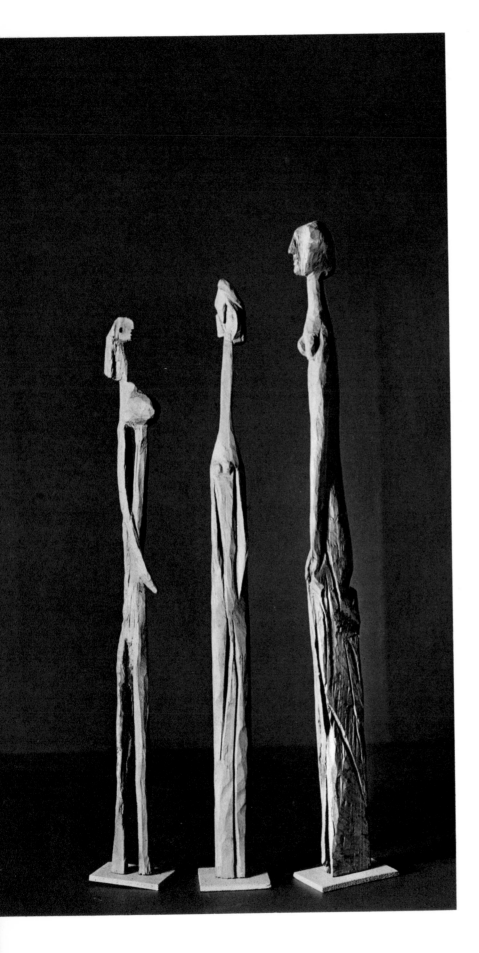

Carved wood, 1931.

Woman. 18⅞ inches high
Woman. 20⅛ inches high
Seated Woman. 21⅞ inches high

Seated Woman. 7⅛ inches high
Seated Woman. 6¾ inches high
Seated Woman. 6¾ inches high
Woman. 7¾ inches high
Woman. 12⅜ inches high

Construction with Glove (By the Sea). 1930. Cardboard, plaster and wood on canvas, covered with sand, 10⅝ x 14 inches

Head of a Woman. 1932. Bronze relief, 27⅛ x 23⅝ inches

Head of a Woman. 1931-1932. Bronze, 19⅝ inches high

BELOW AND OPPOSITE: *Head of a Woman.* 1932. Bronze, 50⅜ inches high

Bust of a Woman. 1932. Bronze, 30¾ inches high

Head of a Woman. 1932. Bronze, 33½ inches high

Head of a Woman. 1932. Bronze, 27½ inches high

Bust of a Woman. 1932. Bronze, 25⅛ inches high

Reclining Woman. 1932. Bronze, 27½ inches long

OPPOSITE: *Seated Woman.* 1931. Bronze, 31⅞ inches high

BELOW: *Heifer's Head*. 1932. Bronze, 13 x 20⅝ x 21¼ inches

OPPOSITE: *Cock*. 1932. Bronze, 26 inches high

84

BELOW, LEFT: *Woman Running.* 1933. Bronze, 20½ inches high

BELOW, RIGHT: *Woman with Raised Arms.* 1932. Bronze,
13 inches high

OPPOSITE: *Woman.* 1931-1932. Bronze, 27⅞ inches high

ABOVE: *Face of a Woman.* 1934. Bronze relief, 11 x 9⅞ inches

LEFT: *Figure.* 1935. Bronze, 22⅞ inches high

OPPOSITE: *Head of a Warrior.* 1933. Bronze, 47⅝ inches high

Woman with Leaves. 1934. Bronze, 15 inches high

OPPOSITE: *Figure.* 1935. Wood, string, and found objects, 44⅛ inches high

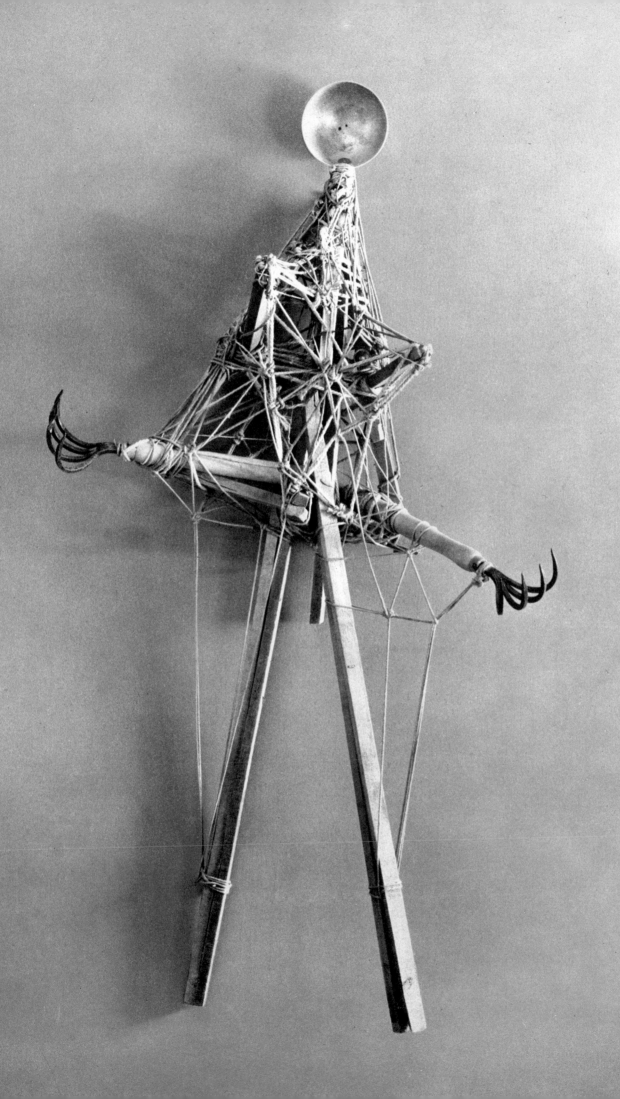

BELOW: *Figure.* 1935. Wood, doll's arm, metal lock, nails, and string on cement base, 13¾ inches high

OPPOSITE.
LEFT: *Articulated Doll.* 1935. Wood and cloth, 20⅞ inches high
RIGHT: *Articulated Doll.* 1935. Wood and cloth, 14⅛ inches high

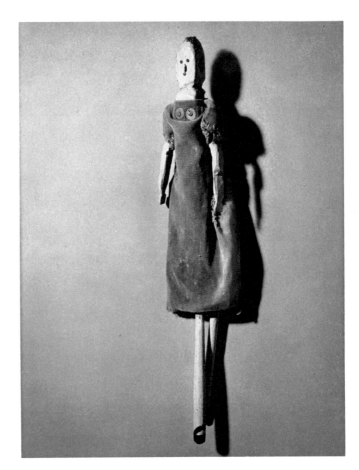

Figure. 1935. Wood, metal, string, and celluloid on cement base, 24¾ inches high

BELOW: *Woman Carrying a Bowl.* 1935. Wood and metal on cement base, 23⅝ inches high

OPPOSITE: *Figure.* 1935. Painted wood on cement base, 23¼ inches high

Construction with Ceramic Tile. 1936. Wood, metal, plaster, and ceramic, 10⅝ inches diameter

OPPOSITE.
ABOVE: *Construction.* 1938. Wood and metal on canvas, 9⅞ x 10⅝ inches
BELOW: *Construction with Flower.* 1938. Wood and metal on canvas, 8¾ x 10⅝ inches

94

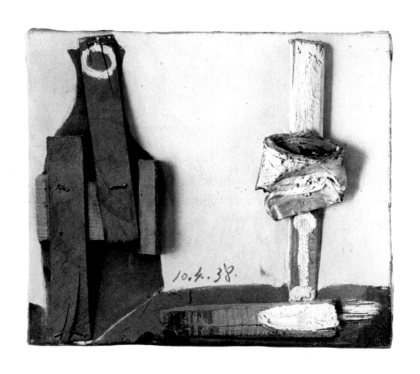

BELOW: *Cat.* 1941. Bronze, 18¼ x 30¼ x 7½ inches

OPPOSITE.
ABOVE: *Cat.* 1944. Bronze, 14⅛ x 21⅝ x 6⅞ inches

BELOW: *Woman Running.* 1940. Bronze, 12⅝ inches high; base diameter, 6¼ inches

97

Woman Leaning on Her Elbow. 1943. Bronze, 24¾ inches high
OPPOSITE: *Figure.* 1944. Bronze, 60½ inches high, on stone base

Head of a Woman. 1943. Bronze, 23¼ inches high

OPPOSITE.

LEFT: *Woman*. 1943. Bronze relief, 20⅞ x 7½ inches

RIGHT: *Reaper*. 1943. Bronze, 20¼ inches high

"*La Madame.*" 1943-1944. Bronze, 67¾ inches high, on stone base

OPPOSITE: *Woman with Apple.* 1943. Bronze, 70⅞ inches high

Flowering Watering Can. 1943-1944. Bronze, 33 inches high

OPPOSITE: *Woman in a Long Dress.* 1943-1944. Bronze, 63⅜ inches high

LEFT AND OPPOSITE: *Man with Sheep.* 1944. Bronze, 86½ inches high

OPPOSITE: *Death's Head (Flayed Head).* 1944. Bronze, 11⅜ x 8⅜ x 10¼ inches
Bull's Head. 1943. Bronze, after bicycle seat and handlebars, 16½ x 16⅛ x 5⅞ inches

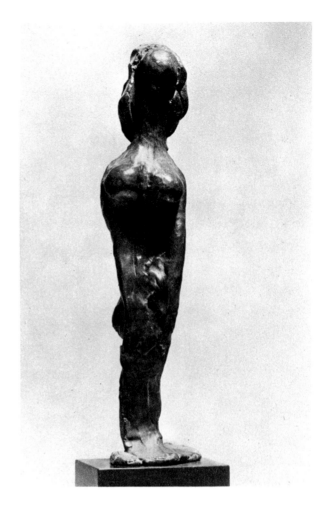

OPPOSITE, BELOW: *Female Figures*. Bronze, 1945, 1947.
Collection Mrs. G. David Thompson, Pittsburgh

Other casts.

LEFT: *Woman*. 1945, 9⅛ inches high

RIGHT: *Woman*. 1945, 9½ inches high

OPPOSITE.

LEFT: *Woman*. 1945, 8⅞ inches high

RIGHT: *Woman*. 1945, 10 inches high

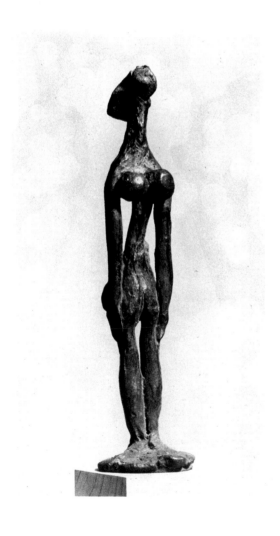

 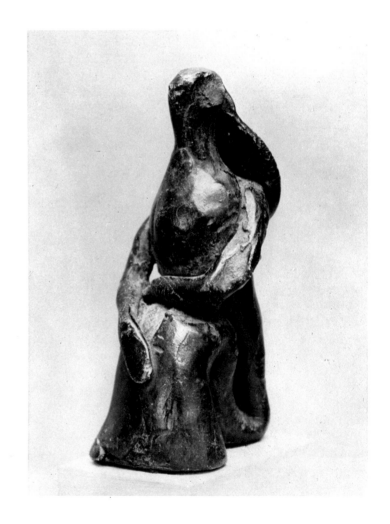

Torso of a Woman. 1946. Bronze, 11 inches high, on wood base

Other casts of figures on p. 110.

OPPOSITE AND LEFT:
Woman. 1945. Bronze, 5¼ inches high
Seated Woman. 1947. Bronze, 4¾ inches high
Woman. 1947. 7⅞ inches high

113

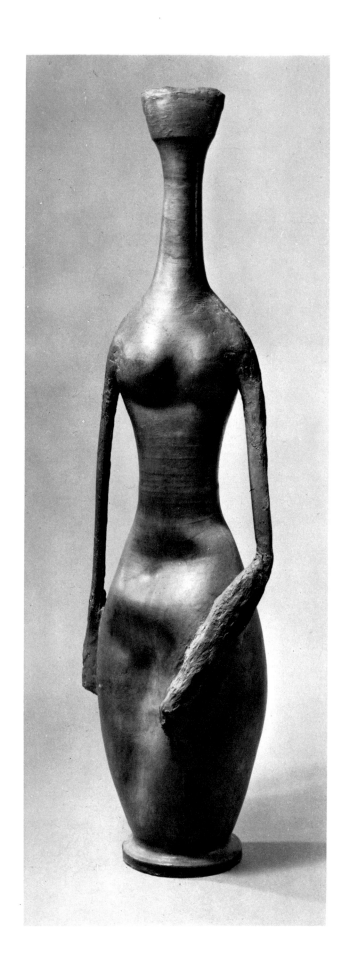

LEFT: *Vase-Woman*. 1948. Bronze, 37¾ inches high
ABOVE: *Woman*. 1947. Bronze, 7¾ inches high
OPPOSITE: *Vase-Face*. 1947. Bronze, 11 inches high
Collection Mrs. G. David Thompson, Pittsburgh

Hand with Sleeve. 1947. Bronze, 9 inches long. Collection Mary and Sylvan Lang, San Antonio, Texas

OPPOSITE: *Female Form*. 1948. Bronze, 50 inches high

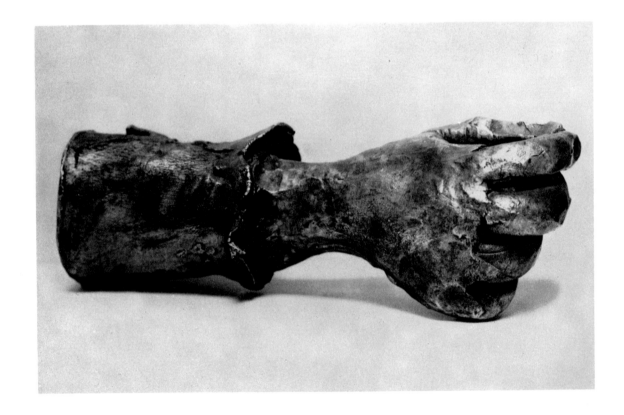

Glass. 1949. Bronze, 8⅜ inches high

BELOW: *Centaur.* 1948. Bronze, 15½ inches high

OPPOSITE.

LEFT: *Animal Head.* 1948. Bronze, 14⅛ inches high

RIGHT: *Mask of a Faun.* 1949-1950. Bronze, 15¾ inches high

ABOVE, LEFT: *Owl*. 1949. Ceramic, 7⅞ x 8¼ x 5¼ inches

ABOVE, RIGHT: *Seated Bird*. 1948. Ceramic, 9¼ x 4¼ x 15⅜ inches

LEFT: *Condor*. 1949. Ceramic, 17 inches high

OPPOSITE, LEFT AND RIGHT: *Woman*. 1948. Ceramic, 14⅞ inches high. Galerie Chalette, New York

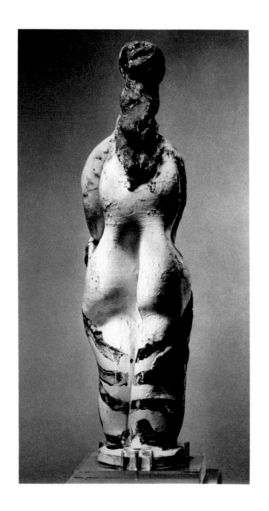 

LEFT: *Woman with Hands Hidden.* 1949. Ceramic, 18½ inches high

RIGHT: *Woman with Mantilla.* 1949. Ceramic, 18½ inches high

OPPOSITE.
ABOVE, LEFT: *Large Sculptured Head.* 1950. Ceramic, 15 inches high

ABOVE, RIGHT: *Large Sculptured Head with Bow.* 1950. Ceramic, 14½ inches high

BELOW, LEFT: *Two-handled Pitcher.* 1950. Ceramic, 13 inches high

BELOW, RIGHT: *Centaur.* 1950. Ceramic, 17 inches high

Mask of a Woman. 1950. Bronze, 10½ inches high

BELOW: *Hand*. 1950. Bronze, 1¾ x 7⅞ inches

OPPOSITE: *Pregnant Woman*. 1950. Bronze, 41¼ inches high.
The Museum of Modern Art, New York,
gift of Mrs. Bertram Smith

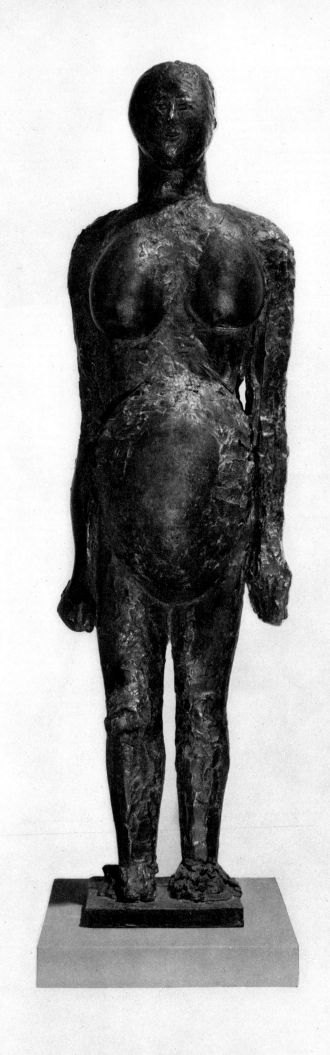

Owl. 1950. Bronze, 13 inches high

BELOW: *Owl.* 1950. Bronze, 14½ inches high

OPPOSITE: *She-Goat.* 1950. Bronze, after found objects,
46⅜ x 56⅜ x 27¾ inches. The Museum of Modern Art,
New York, Mrs. Simon Guggenheim Fund

Little Girl Skipping Rope. 1950. Bronze, after found objects, 60¼ inches high

OPPOSITE: *Woman with Baby Carriage.* 1950. Bronze, after found objects, 80 inches high

Head of a Woman. 1951. Bronze, 21⅛ inches high. The Museum of Modern Art, New York,
Benjamin Scharps and David Scharps Fund

Head of a Woman. 1951. Bronze, 19⅞ inches high

OPPOSITE: *Crane*. 1952. Painted bronze, after found objects, 29½ inches high

Goat Skull and Bottle. 1951-1952. Painted bronze, after found objects, 31 x 37⅝ x 21½ inches.
132   The Museum of Modern Art, New York, Mrs. Simon Guggenheim Fund

ABOVE: *Angry Owl.* 1953. Bronze, after found objects, 10⅞ inches high

BELOW: *Woman Reading.* 1952-1953. Painted bronze, after found objects, 14 inches long.
Collection Mr. and Mrs. Gerald Gidwitz, Highland Park, Illinois

OPPOSITE: *Baboon and Young.* 1951. Bronze, after found objects, 21 inches high.
The Museum of Modern Art, New York, Mrs. Simon Guggenheim Fund

136

Vase with Flower. 1953. Bronze, 29 inches high

BELOW: *Bunch of Flowers.* 1953. Bronze, 23⅝ inches high

OPPOSITE: *Flowers in a Vase.* 1953. Bronze, 28¾ inches high

LEFT: *Kneeling Woman*. 1953. Ceramic, 11⅜ inches high

RIGHT: *Woman*. 1953. Ceramic, 15⅜ inches high

OPPOSITE.

LEFT: *Woman in a Long Dress, Her Hair Undone*.
1953. Ceramic, 11¾ inches high

RIGHT: *Woman*. 1953. Ceramic, 11⅜ inches high

138

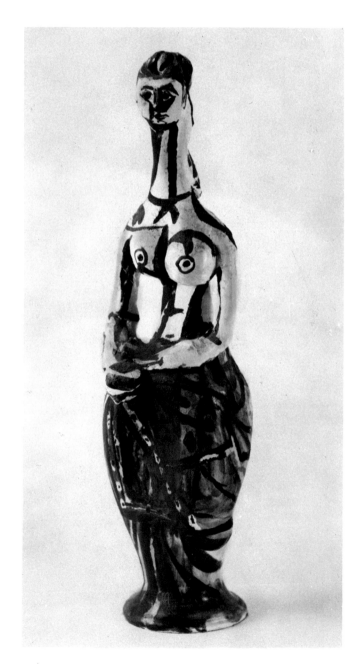

ABOVE: *Owl*. 1953. Ceramic, 13⅝ inches high
BELOW: *Owl*. 1951. Ceramic, 13⅜ inches high

ABOVE: *Owl with Raised Wings.* 1953. Ceramic, 12¼ inches high

BELOW: *Owl with Man's Face (Carnaval).* 1953. Ceramic, 13¾ inches high

ABOVE: *Dove*. 1953. Ceramic, 5½ x 7⅞ x 3¼ inches

BELOW: *Dove*. 1953. Ceramic, 5⅞ x 10¼ x 5⅛ inches

ABOVE: *Dove with Eggs*. 1953. Ceramic, 5½ x 8⅝ x 7⅞ inches

BELOW: *Dove*. 1953. Ceramic, 5⅞ x 9⅞ x 5⅛ inches

Dove. 1953. Ceramic, 4¾ x 8⅝ x 5⅛ inches

BELOW, LEFT: *Two-handled Vase (Great Bird).* 1961. Ceramic, 23¼ inches high

BELOW, RIGHT: *Woman with a Crown of Flowers.* 1954. Ceramic, 9½ inches high. Collection M. and Mme Georges Ramié, Vallauris

143

Dove. 1953. Bronze, 5½ x 9 x 4⅜ inches

CENTER: *Dove.* 1953. Bronze, 6¾ x 11 x 4¾ inches

BELOW: *Little Bull.* 1953. Ceramic, 3½ x 9⅞ x 5⅛ inches

OPPOSITE: *Woman.* 1953. Bronze, 20½ inches high

LEFT: *Woman.* 1953. Painted wood, 54 inches high

RIGHT: *Woman.* 1953. Painted wood, 35½ inches high

OPPOSITE: *Woman Carrying a Child.* 1953. Painted wood, 69 inches high

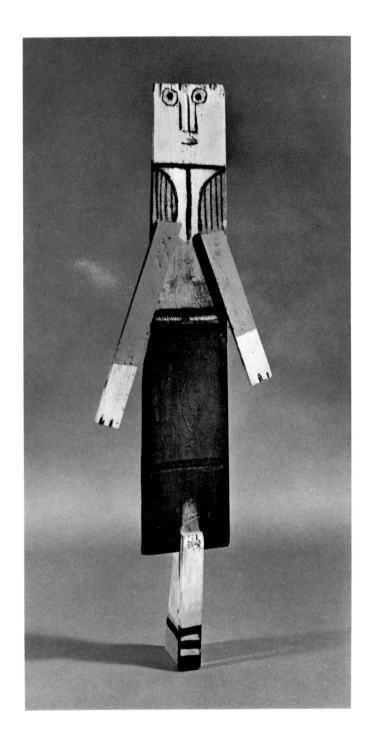

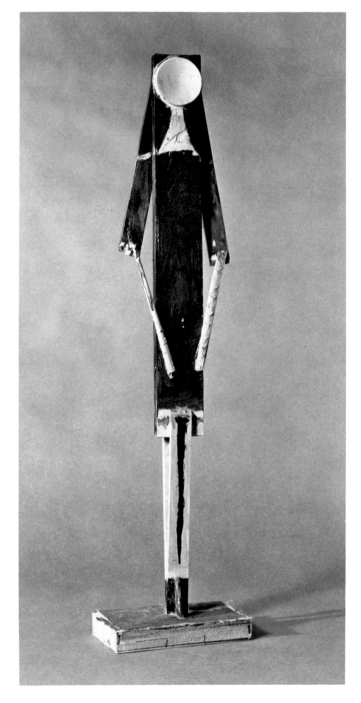

Bust of Sylvette. 1954. Metal cutout, folded and painted, 27½ inches high

OPPOSITE: *Bust of Sylvette*. 1954. Metal cutout, folded and painted, 27⅛ inches high

Bust of Sylvette. 1954. Metal cutout, folded and painted, 24⅜ inches high

Bust of Sylvette. 1954. Metal cutout, folded and painted, 23¼ inches high

Head of a Woman. 1954. Metal cutout, painted, 34¼ inches high

OPPOSITE: *Head of a Woman.* 1954. Metal cutout, painted, 32 inches high

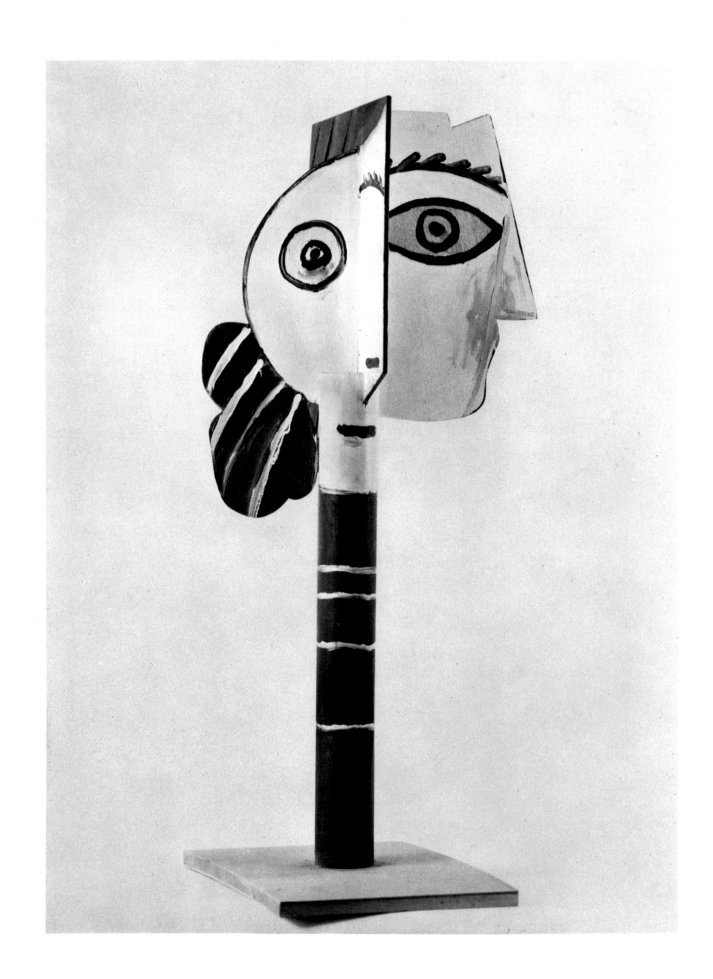

Head of a Woman. 1954. Wood cutout, painted, 31½ inches high

Head of a Woman. 1954. Metal cutout, painted, 30¼ inches high

BELOW: *The Bathers*. 1956. Bronze, after wood. Six figures, the largest 8 feet 8 inches high (not in exhibition)

OPPOSITE: *Young Man*. 1956. Bronze, after wood, 31½ inches high

Bull's Head. 1957. Bronze, 14½ inches high
BELOW: *Bull.* 1957. Bronze, 15¾ x 26 x 8½ inches
OPPOSITE: *Arm.* 1959. Bronze, 22¾ inches high.
Joseph H. Hirshhorn Collection

LEFT: *Bull*. 1958. Bronze, 4¾ inches long. Collection Mr. and Mrs. Victor W. Ganz, New York

RIGHT: *Bull*. 1957. Bronze, 6½ inches long. Collection Larry Aldrich, New York

OPPOSITE.
LEFT: *Pigeon*. 1957. Bronze, 6 x 9⅞ x 4¼ inches

RIGHT: *Head of a Woman with Necklace*. 1957. Bronze, 14¼ inches high

Little Girl. 1957-1958. Painted bronze, 17 inches high
OPPOSITE: *Figure*. 1958. Wood, 53⅛ inches high

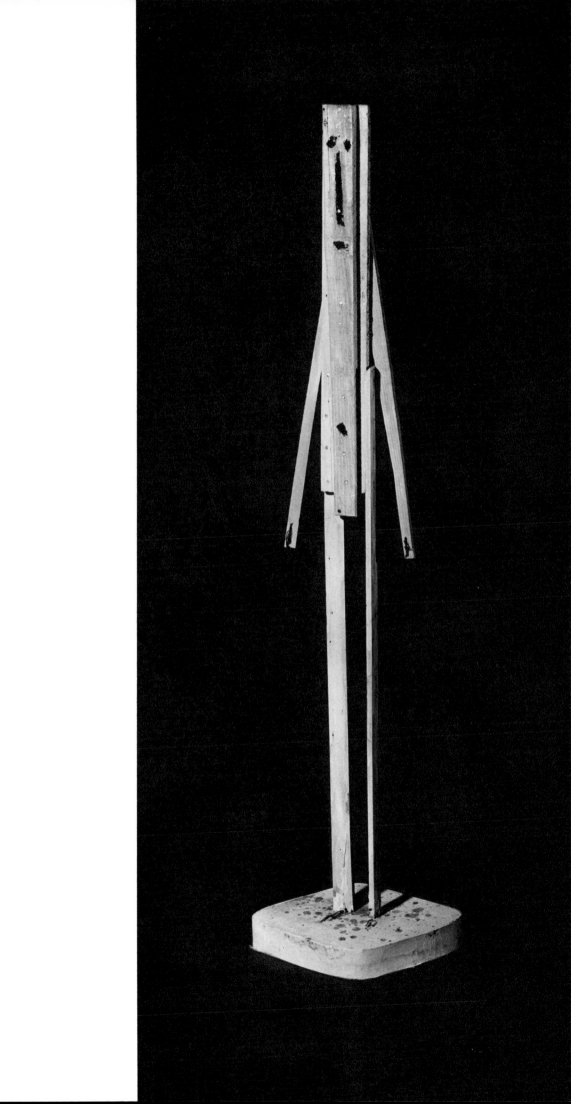

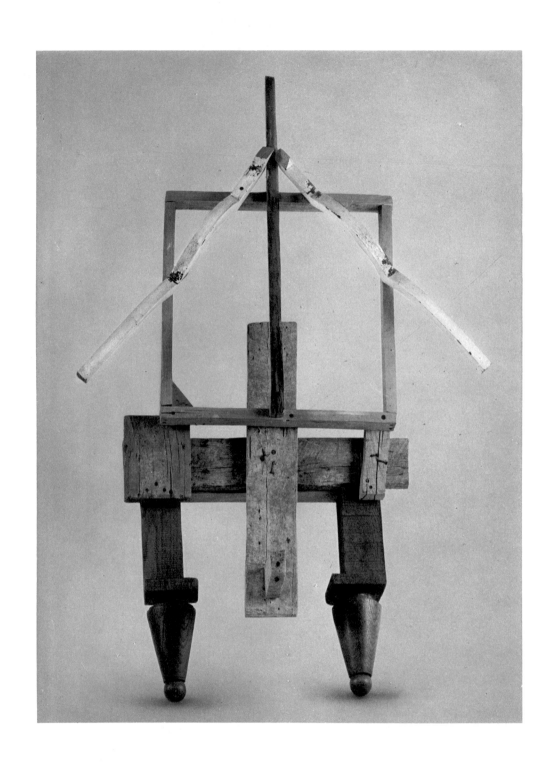

Man. 1958. Wood, 46¾ x 29½ x 11¾ inches

OPPOSITE: *Bather Playing.* 1958. Bronze, after found objects, 44½ inches high

Head. 1958. Bronze, after wood, 20 inches high

Man. 1958. Bronze, after wood, 22½ inches high

Head of a Woman. 1962. Metal cutout, folded and painted, 12⅝ inches high

OPPOSITE: *Head of a Woman with Blonde Hair.* 1958-1959. Painted wood and wicker basket, 32¼ x 21¼ x 2⅜ inches

Figure. 1960. Bronze, after wood and found objects, 48⅜ inches high

Man with Javelin. 1960. Bronze, after wood, 45⅝ inches high

Man Running. 1960. Bronze, 46 inches high

OPPOSITE.

ABOVE, LEFT: *Head of a Woman.* 1961. Bronze, 10⅝ inches high

ABOVE, RIGHT: *Woman.* 1962. Bronze, 12¾ inches high

BELOW, LEFT: *Man with Staff.* 1961. Bronze, 15 inches high

BELOW, RIGHT: *Musician.* 1961. Bronze, 17¾ inches high

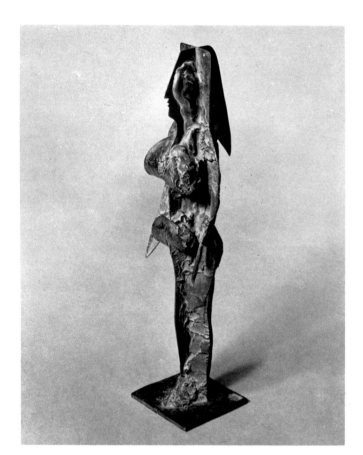

Metal cutouts, folded and painted, 1961.

LEFT: *Woman and Child.* 17¼ inches high

RIGHT: *Woman and Child.* 17¼ inches high

OPPOSITE: *Chair.* 43¾ inches high

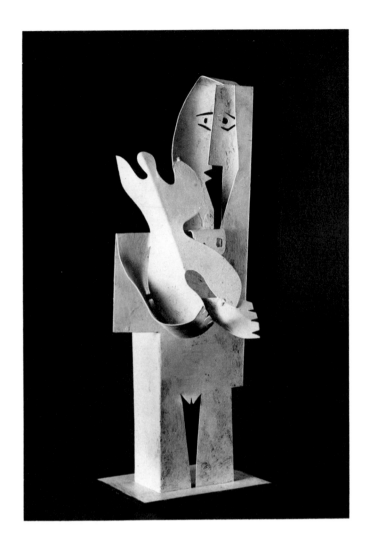

Woman with Bowl. 1961. Metal cutout, folded and painted, 44⅞ inches high

OPPOSITE: *Woman and Child.* 1961. Metal cutout, folded and painted, 50¾ inches high

Metal cutouts, folded and painted, 1961.

ABOVE: *Bust of a Woman*. 12⅞ inches high

LEFT: *Little Monkey*. 6¾ inches high

OPPOSITE.

LEFT: *Head*. 12⅛ inches high

RIGHT: *Woman with Raised Arm*. 13⅜ inches high

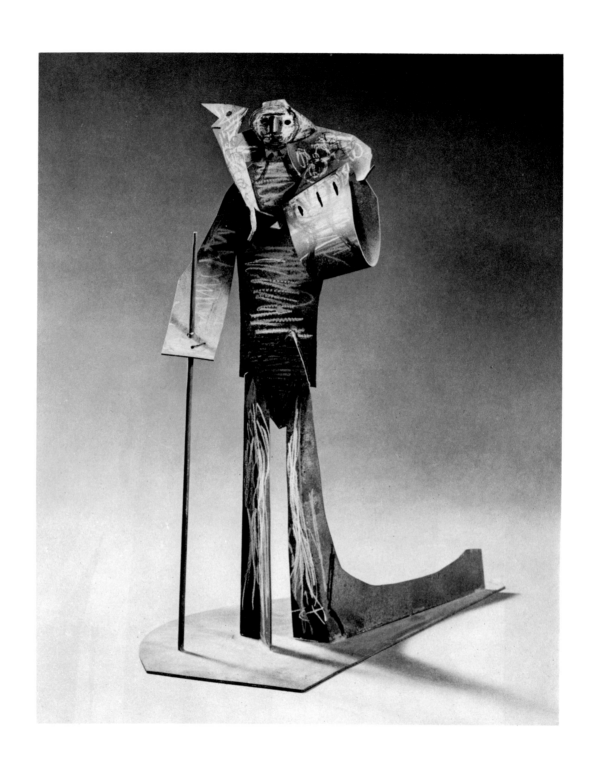

Man with Sheep. 1961. Metal cutout, folded and painted, 20⅞ inches high

Man with Sheep. 1961. Metal cutout, folded and painted, 17¼ inches high

ABOVE: *Owls*. 1961. Metal cutouts, folded and painted. Left, 15 inches high; right, 16⅛ inches high

LEFT: *Sparrow Hawk*. 1960. Metal cutout, 11⅜ inches high

Cock. 1961. Metal cutout, folded and painted, 8⅝ inches high

CENTER: *Bird*. 1961. Metal cutout, folded and painted, 15 inches high

BELOW: *Owl*. 1961. Metal cutout, folded and painted, 9⅞ inches high

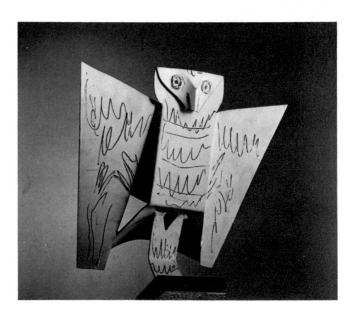

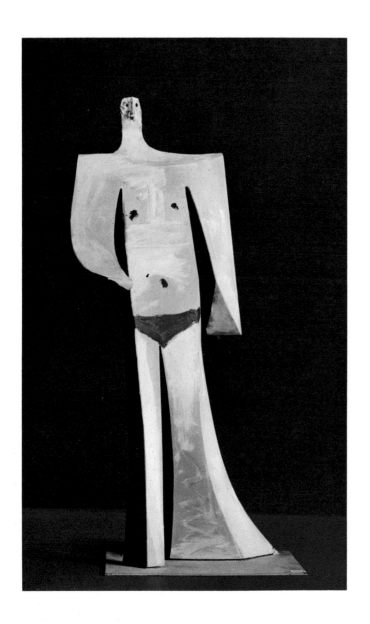

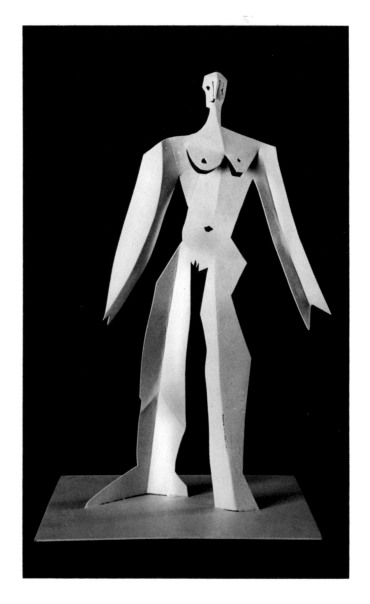

Metal cutouts, folded and painted, 1961.

LEFT: *Bather.* 20⅛ inches high

RIGHT: *Woman.* 17 inches high

OPPOSITE: *Pierrot.* 53⅛ inches high

The Spanish Woman. 1961. Metal cutouts, folded and painted.

LEFT: 6¾ inches high

RIGHT: 8¼ inches high

OPPOSITE: 11 inches high

Head of a Woman. 1961. Metal cutout, folded and painted, 31 ½ inches high

Head of a Bearded Man. 1961. Metal cutout, folded and painted, 31½ inches high

Metal cutouts, folded and painted, 1961.

ABOVE: *Head of a Bearded Man.* 16⅛ inches high

BELOW: *Head of a Bearded Man.* 15 inches high

OPPOSITE.

ABOVE, LEFT: *Head of a Man.* 11 inches high

ABOVE, RIGHT: *Head of a Woman.* 15 inches high

BELOW, LEFT: *Head of a Woman.* 8⅝ inches high

BELOW, RIGHT: *Head of a Woman.* 11 inches high

Woman with Open Arms. 1961. Metal cutout, folded and painted, 11 inches high

BELOW: *Small Woman with Outstretched Arms.* 1961. Metal cutout, folded and painted, 14½ inches high

OPPOSITE: *Woman with Outstretched Arms.* 1961. Metal cutout, folded and painted, 72 inches high

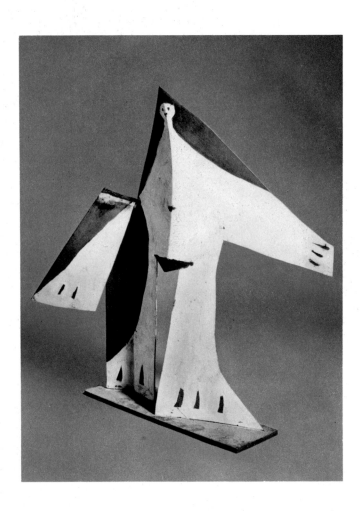

Metal cutouts, folded and painted.

LEFT: *Man with Moustache.* 1962. 11¾ inches high

RIGHT: *Head of a Woman.* 1962. 9⅞ inches high

OPPOSITE.

ABOVE, LEFT: *Football Player.* 1961. 22½ inches high

ABOVE, RIGHT: *Football Player.* 1961. 23¼ inches high

BELOW, LEFT: *Clown.* 1961. 12¼ inches high

BELOW, RIGHT: *Head.* 1961. 6⅝ inches high

 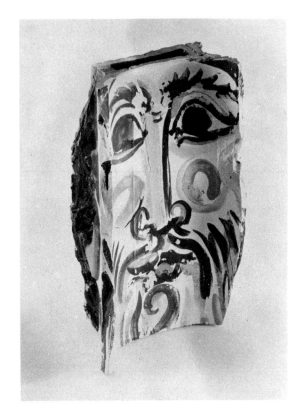

Ceramic (fragments of Roman tile), 1963.

LEFT: *Face.* 8⅝ x 19 inches

RIGHT: *Face.* 19⅞ x 8⅝ inches

OPPOSITE.
Ceramic (fragments of hollow brick), 1962.

ABOVE, LEFT: *Face of a Woman.* 8⅝ x 6¼ x 3⅛ inches

ABOVE, RIGHT: *Face of a Bearded Man.* 8⅝ x 4⅞ x 3⅜ inches

BELOW, LEFT: *Face of a Woman.* 8⅝ x 5⅛ x 3¾ inches

BELOW, RIGHT: *Face of a Woman.* 8⅝ x 4¾ x 3⅛ inches

Jacqueline with a Green Ribbon. 1962. Metal cutout, folded and painted, 20½ inches high

Head of a Woman. 1962. Metal cutout, folded and painted, 19⅝ inches high

Head of a Woman. 1962. Metal cutout, folded and painted, 19⅝ inches high

Head of a Woman. 1962. Metal cutout, folded and painted, 12⅝ inches high

Bust of a Woman. 1962. Metal cutout, folded and painted, 17¾ inches high

Head of a Woman. 1960. Metal cutout, folded and painted, 13¾ inches high

Head of a Woman. 1962. Metal cutout, folded and painted, 19⅝ inches high

Head of a Woman. 1962. Metal cutout, folded and painted, 19⅝ inches high

Head of a Woman. 1962. Metal cutout, folded, 20½ inches high

OPPOSITE: Model for the Chicago Civic Center sculpture. 1965. Welded steel, 41¼ inches high.
The Art Institute of Chicago, gift of Pablo Picasso

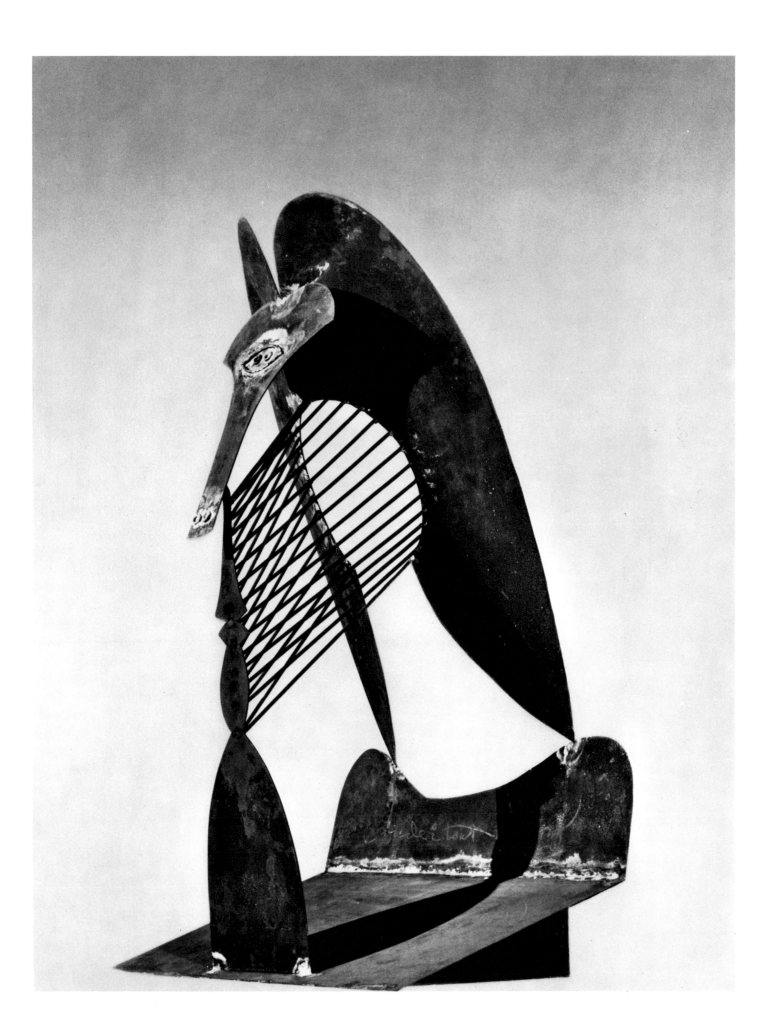

Women with Hat. 1963. Metal cutout, folded and painted, 49½ inches high.
Galerie Claude Bernard, Paris (not in exhibition)

RELATED WORKS

BIBLIOGRAPHY

CATALOGUE OF THE EXHIBITION

1. Iberian stone bas-relief from Osuna. The Louvre

2. *Girl Combing Her Hair*. 1905. Crayon, 22 x 16 inches. Collection Sir Robert and Lady Sainsbury, London

3. *Les Demoiselles d'Avignon*. 1907. Oil on canvas, 8 feet x 7 feet 8 inches. The Museum of Modern Art, New York, acquired through the Lillie P. Bliss Bequest

4. *Figure in Profile*. 1907. Pastel and watercolor, 24¾ x 18⅞ inches

5. *Head of a Woman*. 1909. Conté crayon, 24¾ x 19 inches

6. *Glass and Dice*. 1914. Pasted paper and charcoal, 9½ x 6¾ inches. Heinz Berggruen, Paris

7

7. *The Manager from New York*. Costume designed by Picasso for *Parade,* 1917. From Zervos, *Pablo Picasso,* vol. II, no. 964 (bibl. 16)

8. *Head.* 1928. Construction in painted metal, about 10 inches high. From *Cahiers d'Art,* no. 4, 1929

9. *The Painter and His Model.* 1928. Oil on canvas, 51⅝ x 63⅞ inches. The Museum of Modern Art, New York, fractional gift, Mr. and Mrs. Sidney Janis Collection

10. Page from sketchbook, 1924. Pen and ink. Reproduced in Balzac's *Le Chef d'oeuvre inconnu* (Paris, 1931)

11. *Two Seated Women.* 1920. Oil on canvas, 76¾ x 64¼ inches. Collection Walter P. Chrysler, Jr.

12. Study for *Wire Construction.* 1928. Pen and ink. From Zervos, vol. VII, no. 206

8

9

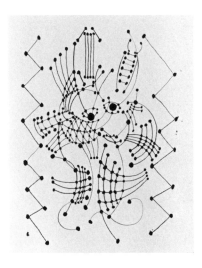

10

11

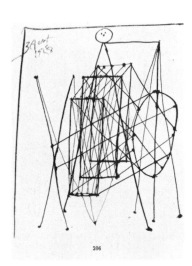

12

13

14

15

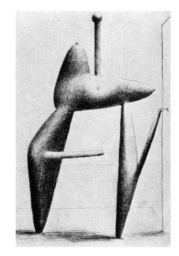

16

17

13. *Head of a Woman (Design for Sculpture)*. 1932. Charcoal on canvas, 36¼ x 28¾ inches. Galerie Beyeler, Basel

14. Detail from *An Anatomy*. 1933. Pencil. From *Minotaure* (Paris), no. 1, 1933

15. *Crucifixion*. 1932. Pen and ink, 13⅜ x 20⅛ inches

16. Page from sketchbook, 1927. *Study for a Monument,* charcoal. From Zervos, vol. VII, no. 92

17. *Metamorphosis*. 1928. Plaster, 8¾ inches high. From *Cahiers d'Art,* no. 7, 1928

18

19

20

21

18. *Head of a Woman (Study for Sculpture).* 1962. Pencil, 16½ x 10⅝ inches. Galerie Louise Leiris, Paris

19. Study for *Man with Sheep.* 1943. Pen and ink, 51⅛ x 20 inches

20. *Head of a Woman.* 1943. Paper, cut out and folded. Photograph: Brassaï

21. Carl Nesjar. *Woman with Outstretched Arms.* 1962. Sandblasted concrete, 20 feet high, from model by Picasso. In garden of D. H. Kahnweiler, Chalo-St. Mars, (S/O) France

Compiled by Inga Forslund

Selected monographs and œuvre catalogues

1 BARR, ALFRED H., JR. *Picasso: Fifty Years of His Art.* New York: The Museum of Modern Art, 1946. 314 pp. illus.
Reprint edition, New York: Arno Press, 1966. Based on *Picasso: Forty Years of His Art* (bibl. 93) with new and greatly amplified text. Statements, extensive bibl.

2 BOECK, WILHELM, and Jaime Sabartés. *Picasso.* New York: Harry N. Abrams, 1955. 524 pp. illus.
Sections on sculpture (pp. 285-292, illus. pp. 432-439) and ceramics (pp. 278-284, illus. pp. 440-451). Extensive bibl.

3 *Cahiers d'Art* (Paris), vol. 23, no. 1, 1948. 208 pp. illus.
Issue devoted to Picasso. Includes "Céramiques de Picasso," by Christian Zervos (pp. 72-73); "Picasso Céramiste," by Madoura [Georges and Suzanne Ramié] (pp. 74-80 illus.); "Picasso à Vallauris," also on ceramics, by Jaime Sabartés (pp. 81-83 illus.); further illus. of 446 ceramics, pp. 84-208.

4 CHAMPRIS, PIERRE DE. *Picasso: ombre et soleil.* Paris: Gallimard, 1960. 295 pp. illus.
Sculpture and ceramics pp. 226-236, illus.

5 DAIX, PIERRE. *Picasso.* New York: Frederick A. Praeger, 1965. 271 pp. illus. ("Praeger World of Art Profiles").
Separate section on ceramics (pp. 198-202). Translated from the French, Paris: Editions Aimery Somogy, 1964.

6 ELGAR, FRANK, and Robert Maillard. *Picasso.* New York: Frederick A. Praeger, 1956. 314 pp. illus., bibl.
"A study of the work by Frank Elgar. A biographical study by Robert Maillard." Translated from the French, Paris: Fernand Hazan, 1955.

7 GIEURE, MAURICE. *Initiation à l'œuvre de Picasso.* Paris: Editions des Deux Mondes, 1951. 337 pp. plus 142 illus.
Includes "Les Sculptures de Picasso" (pp. 143-159).

8 JANIS, HARRIET and SIDNEY. *Picasso: The Recent Years 1939-1946.* Garden City, New York: Doubleday & Company, 1946. 211 pp. illus.

9 LA SOUCHÈRE, DOR DE. *Picasso in Antibes.* New York: Pantheon Books, 1960. 68 pp. plus 99 illus.
Photographs by Marianne Greenwood. "Official catalogue of the Musée d'Antibes, known as the Musée Picasso" (*see* page 45). Includes 2 sculptures and 77 ceramics. Translated from the French.

MAILLARD, ROBERT. *See* bibl. 6.

10 MERLI, JOAN. *Picasso, el artista y la obra de nuestro tiempo.*

2nd edition. Buenos Aires: Poseidon, 1948. 607 pp. illus., plus 37 pl.
Especially extensive illus. (704 black and white, 37 color). First edition 1942.

11 PARMELIN, HÉLÈNE. *Picasso: Women. Cannes and Mougins, 1954-1963.* London: Weidenfeld and Nicolson, 1965. 199 pp. illus.
Preface by Douglas Cooper. Translated from the French, Paris: Cercle d'Art, 1964.

12 PENROSE, ROLAND. *Picasso: His Life and Work.* London: Victor Gollancz, 1958. 392 pp. plus illus., bibl.

13 QUINN, EDWARD, and Roland Penrose. *Picasso at Work: An Intimate Photographic Study.* Garden City, New York: Doubleday & Company, 1964. 16 pp. plus 282 illus.
Photographs by Edward Quinn. Introduction and text by Roland Penrose.

14 RAYNAL, MAURICE. *Picasso.* New York: Skira, 1953. 135 pp. illus., chron., bibl. ("The Taste of Our Time," 4).
Section on ceramics pp. 117-119 illus. Translated from the French, Geneva: Skira, 1953.

SABARTÉS, JAIME. *See* bibl. 2.

15 *Verve* (Paris), vol. 7, no. 25/26, 1951. 96 pp. illus.
Issue devoted to Picasso's work at Vallauris, 1949-1951. Includes "Equivalences chez Picasso," on the sculpture, by Odysseus Elytis (pp. [28-39] illus.); and "Céramiques," by Georges Ramié (pp. [40-84] illus.). Re-issued with inserted English translation as *Picasso at Vallauris,* New York: Reynal and Company, 1959.

16 ZERVOS, CHRISTIAN. *Pablo Picasso: Oeuvres de....* Paris: Cahiers d'Art, 1932-1966. 17 vols. illus.
Oeuvre catalogue of works from 1895 to 1957; not complete for sculpture or ceramics. Still in publication.

Books and articles on the sculpture

ARAGON, LOUIS. *See* bibl. 97.

17 ARGAN, GIULIO CARLO. "Cubismo e surrealismo nella scultura di Picasso," *Letteratura* (Rome), vol. 1, no. 4, 1953, pp. 11-16.

18 ———. *Scultura di Picasso.* Venice: Alfieri, 1953. 34 pp. plus illus.
Italian text followed by English translation.

BARR, ALFRED H., JR. *See* bibl. 1, 93.

BOECK, WILHELM. *See* bibl. 2.

BOGGS, JEAN SUTHERLAND. *See* bibl. 117.

19 Brassaï [Jules Halasz]. *Picasso and Company.* Garden City, New York: Doubleday & Company, 1966. 289 pp. plus 57 illus.
    Preface by Henry Miller. Introduction by Roland Penrose. Photographs by the author. Translated from the French, *Conversations avec Picasso,* Paris: Gallimard, 1964.

20 Breton, André. "Picasso dans son élément," *Minotaure* (Paris), no. 1, 1933, pp. 8-29 illus.
    Largely photographs by Brassaï.

Champris, Pierre de. *See* bibl. 4.

21 Chevalier, Denys. "Propos autour d'une sculpture de Picasso," *Arts de France* (Paris), no. 8, 1946, pp. 77-79 illus.
    On *Woman with Apple* (page 103).

22 "The Chicago Picasso," *Progressive Architecture* (New York), Nov. 1966, p. 66 illus.
    On sculpture for the Civic Center (page 207).

Daix, Pierre. *See* bibl. 5.

23 D[avis], R[ichard] S. "Sculpture by Painters: Picasso," *Minneapolis Institute of Arts Bulletin,* May/June 1956, pp. 34-35 illus.

24 E[lgar], F[rank]. "Picasso," in *Dictionary of Modern Sculpture,* Robert Maillard, ed. New York: Tudor, 1960, pp. 239-242 illus.
    _____. *See also* bibl. 6.

Elytis, Odysseus. *See* bibl. 15.

25 Fermigier, André. "Picasso in Paris," *Burlington Magazine* (London), Apr. 1967, pp. 246-247.
    On the occasion of exhibition *Hommage à Pablo Picasso* (bibl. 122).

26 Gaffe, René. "Sculpteur, Picasso?" *Artes* (Antwerp), ser. 2, no. 3/4, 1947/1948, pp. 36-37.
    In issue devoted to Picasso, on occasion of exhibition at Galerie Artes, Antwerp.

Gascar, Pierre. *See* bibl. 121.

Gervis, Daniel. *See* bibl. 121.

27 Giedion-Welcker, Carola. *Contemporary Sculpture: An Evolution in Volume and Space.* 2nd edition. New York: George Wittenborn, 1960, pp. 346-347 and passim. ("Documents of Modern Art," 12).
    First edition 1955.

Gieure, Maurice. *See* bibl. 7.

28 Gischia, L[éon], and N[icole] Védrès. *La sculpture en France depuis Rodin.* Paris: Editions du Seuil, 1945, pp. 146-148 illus.

29 Golding, John. *Cubism: A History and an Analysis, 1907-1914.* New York: George Wittenborn, 1959, pp. 81-83.

30 Gonzalez, J[ulio]. "Picasso sculpteur. Exposition des sculptures récentes de Picasso: Galerie 'Cahiers d'Art'," *Cahiers d'Art* (Paris), vol. 11, no. 6/7, 1936, pp. 189-191 illus.

31 Gueguen, Pierre. "La sculpture cubiste," *Art d'Aujourd'hui* (Paris), ser. 4, no. 3/4, 1953, pp. 50-58.

32 Hahn, Otto. "The Picasso Enigma," *Art and Artists* (London), Feb. 1967, pp. 20-25 illus.

33 Henze, Anton. "Neue Plastiken von Picasso," *Kunstwerk* (Baden-Baden), Mar. 1960, pp. 17-26 illus.
    Includes brief summary in English, opposite p. 1.

Janis, Harriet and Sidney. *See* bibl. 8.

34 Kahnweiler, Daniel-Henry. *Les Sculptures de Picasso.* Paris: Editions du Chêne, 1948. [13] pp. plus 216 pl.
    Photographs by Brassaï. English edition, translated by A.D.B. Sylvester, London: Rodney Phillips, 1949.

35 Laporte, Paul M. "The Man with the Lamb," *Art Journal* (New York), Spring 1962, pp. 144-150 illus.
    On *Man with Sheep* (pages 106-107).

36 Laughton, Bruce. "Picasso," *Arts Review* (London), June 10, 1967, p. 199 illus.
    On the occasion of Arts Council of Great Britain exhibition (bibl. 126).

37 Leymarie, Jean. "Hommage à Picasso: Expositions au Grand Palais et au Petit Palais," *La Revue du Louvre et des Musées de France* (Paris), vol. 16, no. 6, 1966, pp. 291-316 illus.
    Sculpture, pp. 312-315 illus. Ceramics pp. 315-316. *See also* bibl. 122.

38 Lieberman, William S. *The Sculptor's Studio: Etchings by Picasso.* New York: The Museum of Modern Art, 1952. [4] pp. plus 24 pl.

Maillard, Robert. *See* bibl. 6.

Merli, Joan. *See* bibl. 10.

Nesjar, Carl. *See* bibl. 121, 123, 125.

Parmelin, Hélène. *See* bibl. 11.

39 Penrose, Roland. "Espaço e volume na escultura contemporânea," *Cóloquio* (Lisbon), Feb. 1960, pp. 1-8 illus.

40 _____. "A Monumental Sculpture by Picasso in Chicago," *ICA* [Institute of Contemporary Arts, London] *Bulletin,* Nov. 1966, pp. 14-15 illus.
    On the Chicago Civic Center sculpture (page 207).

41 _____. *Picasso.* New York: Universe Books, 1961. [13] pp. plus 32 pl., biog., bibl. ("Universe Sculpture Series").

42 _____. *Picasso: Sculptures.* New York: Tudor, 1965 [16] pp. plus 24 pl. ("Little Art Library," 72).
    Translated from the French, Paris: Fernand Hazan, 1965. ("Petite encyclopédie de l' art").
    _____. *See also* bibl. 12, 13, 126.

43 P[orter], F[airfield]. "Picasso Also as a Sculptor," *Art News* (New York), Mar. 1952, p. 26 illus.

44 Prampolini, Enrico. *Picasso scultore.* Rome: Libreria Fra-

telli Bocca, 1943. 31 pp. illus. ("Anticipazioni," 2: "Serie Arti").

45 PREJGER, LIONEL. "Picasso découpe le fer," *L'Oeil* (Paris), Oct. 1961, pp. 28-33.

QUINN, EDWARD. *See* bibl. 13.

46 READ, HERBERT. *The Art of Sculpture*. New York: Pantheon Books, 1956, pp. 102, 111, 122; pl. 53, 191. ("Bollingen Series," 35: 3).

47 RIEDL, PETER ANSELM. "'Masque d'homme', ein Frühwerk Pablo Picassos," *Jahrbuch der Hamburger Kunstsammlungen*, vol. 7, 1962, pp. 83-92 illus.
On *Mask of a Picador with a Broken Nose* (page 51).

48 RITCHIE, ANDREW CARNDUFF. *Sculpture of the Twentieth Century*. New York: The Museum of Modern Art, 1952, pp. 25-28, 29, 31-32, 231, plus illus.

49 ROSENBLUM, ROBERT. *Cubism and Twentieth-Century Art*. New York: Harry N. Abrams, 1960, pp. 262-268 illus.

SABARTÉS, JAIME. *See* bibl. 2.

50 SALLES, GEORGES A. "Les baigneurs de Picasso," *Quadrum* (Brussels), no. 5, 1958, pp. 4-10 illus.
Brief summary in English, p. 187.

51 "Sculpture monumentale de Picasso dans la région parisienne," *Aujourd'hui* (Boulogne), Sept. 1962, pp. 12-13 illus.

52 SEUPHOR, MICHEL. *The Sculpture of This Century*. New York: George Braziller, 1960, pp. 318-319 and passim.
Translated from the French, Neuchâtel: Editions du Griffon, 1959.

53 SWEENEY, JAMES JOHNSON. "Picasso and Iberian Sculpture," *Art Bulletin* (New York), Sept. 1941, pp. 191-198 plus 4 pl.

VÉDRÈS, N[ICOLE]. *See* bibl. 28.

54 VERDET, ANDRÉ. *La chèvre*. Paris: Editions de Beaune, 1952. [27] pp. illus.
On *She-Goat* (page 126).

55 ———. *Faunes et nymphes de Pablo Picasso*. Geneva: Pierre Cailler, 1952. 39 pp. plus 32 illus. ("Peintres et sculpteurs d'hier et d'aujourd'hui," 25).

56 ———. *L'homme au mouton de Pablo Picasso*. Paris: Falaize, 1950. 24 pp. plus 22 illus.
Poem read at installation of *Man with Sheep* (pages 106-107) in Vallauris, Aug. 6, 1950 (page 45).

57 VERONESI, GIULIA. "Sculture di Picasso," *Emporium* (Bergamo), Apr. 1951, pp. 146-153 illus.
Verve. See bibl. 15.

58 ZERVOS, CHRISTIAN. "L'homme à l'agneau de Picasso," *Cahiers d'Art* (Paris), vol. 20/21, 1945/1946, pp. 84-112 illus.
On *Man with Sheep* (pages 106-107).

59 ———. "Projets de Picasso pour un monument," *Cahiers d'Art* (Paris), vol. 4, no. 8/9, 1929, pp. 342-344 plus 10 illus.
In same volume, "Picasso à Dinard," pp. 5-21 illus.

60 ———. "Sculptures des peintres d'aujourd'hui," *Cahiers d'Art* (Paris), vol. 3, no. 7, 1928, pp. 276-[289] illus.

———. *See also* bibl. 16, 99.

Books and articles on the ceramics

61 BALLARDINI, GAETANO. "Picasso a Faenza," *Faenza*, vol. 36, no. 3, 1950, pp. 47-48, plus illus.

62 BATIGNE, RENÉE. *Une visite à Vallauris: Guide illustré*. Vallauris: Editions du Musée de Vallauris, 1950. [62] pp. illus.
Preface by Georges A. Salles. Includes chapter on the museum, and "Extraits de l'ouvrage céramiques de Picasso" by Madoura [Georges and Suzanne Ramié].

BOECK, WILHELM. *See* bibl. 2.

63 BOURET, JEAN. "Picasso, potier," *Arts* (Paris), Nov. 26, 1948, p. 4.

Cahiers d'Art. See bibl. 3.

64 CASSOU, JEAN. "Les poteries de Picasso," *Art & Décoration* (Paris), no. 12, 1949, pp. 13-21 illus.

65 CHAMPIGNEULLE, BERNARD. "Picasso: poteries nouvelles," *Art & Décoration* (Paris), Nov. 1958, pp. 23-25 illus.

CHAMPRIS, PIERRE DE. *See* bibl. 4.

DAIX, PIERRE. *See* bibl. 5.

ELGAR, FRANK. *See* bibl. 6.

66 GHEERBRANT, B. "Picasso 'Pâtes blanches': New Clay Casts from Original Plaster Moulds," *Graphis* (Zurich), May/June 1957, pp. 240-243, 277-279 illus.
Text in English, French, and German.

67 GOLFIERI, ENNIO. "Le ceramiche di Picasso al Museo di Faenza," *Bolletino d'Arte* (Rome), Jan./Mar. 1952, pp. 21-25 illus.

68 GRAND, P. M. "Céramiques de peintres," *Art & Décoration* (Paris), no. 30, 1952, pp. 4-7 illus.

HERING, KARL-HEINZ. *See* bibl. 115.

69 JOUFFROY, ALAIN. "Ceramics and Small Sculptures by Painters," *Graphis* (Zurich), May/June 1957, pp. 236-239, 280 illus.
Text in English, French, and German.

70 KAHNWEILER, DANIEL-HENRY. *Picasso: Keramik. Ceramic. Céramiques*. Hanover: Schmidt-Küster, 1957. 127 pp. illus.
Text in English, French, and German.

LA SOUCHÈRE, DOR DE. *See* bibl. 9.

71 LEVY, MERVYN. "The Pure Joy: Picasso Ceramics, Arts Council," *Art News and Review* (London), May 11, 1957, p. 6.
On occasion of ceramics exhibition at the Arts Council of Great Britain (*see* bibl. 107).

LEYMARIE, JEAN. *See* bibl. 37, 122.

LIVERANI, GIUSEPPE. *See* bibl. 114.

MADOURA. *See* bibl. 3, 62, 82, 110, 120.

MAILLARD, ROBERT. *See* bibl. 6.

72 MOUTARD-ULDRY, RENÉE. "Les poteries de Picasso," *Art et Industrie* (Paris), no. 14, 1949, pp. 43-45 illus.

73 _____. "La renaissance de la céramique à Vallauris," *Cahiers de la Céramique et des Arts du Feu* (Sèvres), June 1956, pp. 21-29 illus.

74 _____. "Vallauris: Picasso et les potiers précolombiens," *Arts* (Paris), Sept. 7-13, 1955, p. 8 illus.

75 NEWTON, ERIC. "Picasso as Potter," *Art News and Review* (London), Oct. 2, 1954, pp. 1, 8.

76 NIELSEN, JAIS. "Picassos keramik," *Dansk Kunsthaandvaerk* (Copenhagen), June 1950, pp. 101-105 illus.

77 OUVALIEV, DORA. "Picasso's Pottery," *Art News and Review* (London), Mar. 26, 1949, pp. 26-27 illus.

PARMELIN, HÉLÈNE. *See* bibl. 11, 110.

PENROSE, ROLAND. *See* bibl. 12, 13, 126.

78 "Picasso convertirà alla ceramica," *Domus* (Milan), no. 226, 1948, pp. 24-26 illus.

79 "Picassos Keramik," *Du* (Zurich), Oct. 1953, pp. 46-50 illus.

80 "Les poteries de Picasso," *Esprit* (Paris), Feb. 1949, p. 290.

QUINN, EDWARD. *See* bibl. 13.

81 RAMIÉ, GEORGES. *Picasso: Pottery*. New York: Tudor, 1962. 15 pp. plus 15 pl. ("Little Art Library," 48).
    Translated from the French, Paris: Fernand Hazen, 1962. ("Petite encyclopédie de l'art").

    _____. *See also* bibl. 15, 115.

82 RAMIÉ, GEORGES and SUZANNE. *The Ceramics of Picasso*. New York: Skira, 1955. 18 pp. plus 18 pl.
    Translated from the French, Paris: Albert Skira, 1948. Excerpts reprinted in *Craft Horizons* (New York), Summer 1950, pp. 10-13 illus.

    _____. *See also* bibl. 3, 62, 110, 120.

RAYNAL, MAURICE. *See* bibl. 14.

83 RÖTHEL, HANS K. "Töpferarbeiten von Pablo Picasso," *Die Kunst und das schöne Heim* (Munich), Apr. 1949, pp. 15-18 illus.

84 SABARTÉS, JAIME. *Picasso ceramista*. Milan: All'Insegna del Pesce d'Oro, 1953. [31] pp. illus. ("All'Insegna del Pesce d'Oro," 43: "Seria illustrata," Vanni Schweiwiller, ed.).
    Booklet, translated from the Spanish.

    _____. *See also* bibl. 2, 3.

85 TALLON, W. J. "An Art Critic Looks at: Picasso's Pottery," *Design* (Columbus, Ohio), Nov. 1949, pp. 17, 21, 24 illus.

86 TOESCA, MAURICE. "Picasso, céramiste," *Age Nouveau* (Paris), Feb. 1949, p. 100 plus 1 pl.

87 VALLIER, DORA. "Picasso: nouvelles céramiques," *XXe Siècle* (Paris), Noël 1963, pp. [113-116] illus.

88 VALSECCHI, MARCO. "Le ceramiche di Picasso," *Biennale di Venezia*, Apr./June 1953, pp. 31-35 illus.
    In issue on Picasso, occasioned by exhibition at Galleria Nazionale d'Arte Moderna, Rome (bibl. 100).

VERDET, ANDRÉ. *See* bibl. 115.

89 VERONESI, GIULIA. "Le ceramiche di Picasso," *Emporium* (Bergamo), May, 1950, pp. 207-210 illus.

Verve. See bibl. 15.

90 ZERVOS, CHRISTIAN. "Céramiques de Picasso." *See* bibl. 3.
    Reprinted in English, French, and German in *Graphis* (Zurich), vol. 5, no. 27, 1949, pp. 260-269, 298, 301-302 illus.

    _____. *See also* bibl. 16.

91 ZUCKER, PAUL. "Clay and Color: The Ceramics of Picasso." Unpublished typescript. 6 pp.
    Transcription of talk delivered Mar. 27, 1958 on the occasion of the exhibition at Cooper Union Museum, New York (*see* bibl. 111). Copy in Library, The Museum of Modern Art, New York.

Selected exhibition catalogues
(arranged chronologically)

1932

92 PARIS. GALERIES GEORGES PETIT. *Exposition Picasso*. June 16–July 30, 1932. 77 pp. plus 32 pl.
    236 works (7 sculptures, none reproduced). Documentation compiled by Charles Vrancken.

1939-1940

93 NEW YORK. THE MUSEUM OF MODERN ART. *Picasso: Forty Years of His Art*. Alfred H. Barr, Jr., ed. Nov. 15, 1939–Jan. 7, 1940. 207 pp. illus.
    300 works (4 sculptures, all reproduced, and reproductions of 2 not exhibited). Exhibition arranged in collaboration with The Art Institute of Chicago, and shown there Feb. 1–Mar. 3, 1940. Also circulated to several other museums in the United States.

1944

94 PARIS. SOCIÉTÉ DU SALON D'AUTOMNE. *Catalogue des ouvrages de peinture, sculpture, dessin, gravure, architecture et art décoratif, exposés au Palais des Beaux Arts de la Ville de Paris*. Oct. 6–Nov. 5, 1944. 61 pp.
    Picasso, p. 61 (5 sculptures, 74 paintings).

1949

95 NEW YORK. BUCHHOLZ GALLERY. *Pablo Picasso: Recent Work*. Mar. 8–Apr. 2, 1949. [16] pp. illus.
    58 works (24 bronzes of 1945-1947, 20 reproduced).

1950

96 LONDON. ARTS COUNCIL OF GREAT BRITAIN. *Picasso in Provence.* Nov.–Dec. 1950. 12 pp. illus.

83 works (24 bronzes, 21 ceramics, 6 reproduced). Foreword by Philip James.

1950-1951

97 PARIS. MAISON DE LA PENSÉE FRANÇAISE. *Picasso: Sculptures. Dessins. 1950-51.* 34 pp. illus.

43 sculptures (8 reproduced). Text by Louis Aragon.

1952

98 NEW YORK. CURT VALENTIN GALLERY. *Pablo Picasso: Paintings, Sculptures, Drawings.* Feb. 19–Mar. 15, 1952. [14] pp. illus.

56 works (10 sculptures, 6 reproduced; 6 ceramics, 2 reproduced).

1953

99 LYON. MUSÉE. *Picasso: Exposition organisée sous l'égide du Syndicat d'Initiative de Lyon.* 2nd edition, 1953. [54] pp. plus 21 illus.

179 works (20 sculptures, 12 ceramics, none reproduced). Includes: "Picasso et l'Espagne," by Jean Cassou; "Picasso et le cubisme," by Daniel-Henry Kahnweiler; "L'arrière-saison de Picasso," by Christian Zervos; "Humanité de Picasso," by René Jullian; "Le savoir voir," by Marcel Michaud.

100 ROME. GALLERIA NAZIONALE D'ARTE MODERNA. *Mostra di Pablo Picasso.* May–July 5, 1953. Rome: De Luca. 69 pp. plus 171 pl.

246 works (32 sculptures, all reproduced; 39 ceramics, none reproduced). Catalogue by Lionello Venturi, with the collaboration of Eugenio Battisti and Nello Ponente. Introduction by Venturi. Chron., bibl.

101 MILAN. PALAZZO REALE. *Pablo Picasso.* Sept.–Nov. 1953. Milan: Amilcare Pizzi. 116 pp. plus 236 illus.

329 works (32 sculptures, 14 reproduced; and 41 ceramics, 5 reproduced). Introduction by Franco Russoli. Chron., bibl.

102 NEW YORK. CURT VALENTIN GALLERY. *Pablo Picasso: 1950-1953.* Nov. 24–Dec. 19, 1953. 30 pp. illus.

65 works (18 sculptures, 10 reproduced; 6 ceramics, 1 reproduced). Includes "Picasso, Good Master of Liberty," by Paul Eluard, translated by Roland Penrose.

1955

103 LONDON. MARLBOROUGH FINE ART, LTD. *Picasso: 63 Drawings 1953-54. 10 Bronzes 1945-1953.* May–June 1955. 11 pp. plus illus.

4 bronzes reproduced. Introduction by Rebecca West.

104 MUNICH. HAUS DER KUNST. *Picasso 1900-1955.* Oct. 25–Dec. 18, 1955. 366 pp. illus.

256 works (35 sculptures, 7 reproduced; 13 ceramics, 4 reproduced). Introduction by Maurice Jardot. Extensive chron. and bibl. Exhibition also shown in Cologne and Hamburg.

1956

105 NEW YORK. GALERIE CHALETTE. *Picasso: "The Woman." Paintings, Drawings, Bronzes, Lithographs.* Apr. 16–May 19, 1956. [20] pp. illus.

32 works (5 bronzes, all reproduced).

1957

106 NEW YORK. FINE ARTS ASSOCIATES. *Picasso: Sculptures.* Part 1. Jan. 15–Feb. 9, 1957. [13] pp. illus.

26 works (17 reproduced). Includes "The Sculptures of Picasso," by Daniel-Henry Kahnweiler (excerpt from bibl. 34).

107 ROTTERDAM. MUSEUM BOYMANS. *Picasso ceramiek.* July 1957. [36] pp. illus.

74 works (29 reproduced). Enlargement of exhibition at the Arts Council of Great Britain, London.

108 NEW YORK. THE MUSEUM OF MODERN ART. *Picasso: 75th Anniversary Exhibition.* Alfred H. Barr, Jr., ed. May 22–Sept. 8, 1957. 116 pp. illus.

295 works (45 sculptures, 36 reproduced; 2 ceramics, both reproduced). Also shown at the Art Institute of Chicago, Oct. 29–Dec. 8, 1957, and (with the addition of prints, illustrated books, and further ceramics) at the Philadelphia Museum of Art in 1958 (*see* bibl. 109).

1958

109 PHILADELPHIA. MUSEUM OF ART. *Picasso: A Loan Exhibition of His Paintings, Drawings, Sculptures, Ceramics, Prints, and Illustrated Books.* Jan. 8–Feb. 23, 1958. 144 pp. illus.

573 works (46 sculptures, 13 reproduced; 75 ceramics, 13 reproduced). Preface by Henry Clifford. Exhibition expanded from *Picasso: 75th Anniversary Exhibition* (*see* bibl. 108) by the addition of ceramics shown in Rotterdam and London (*see* bibl. 107).

110 PARIS. MAISON DE LA PENSÉE FRANÇAISE. *Picasso: cent cinquante céramiques originales.* Mar. 8–June 30, 1958. 59 pp. illus.

Includes "La terre et le feu de Picasso," by Hélène Parmelin; and text by Georges and Suzanne Ramié.

111 NEW YORK. COOPER UNION MUSEUM. *Ceramics by Picasso.* Mar. 28–May 10, 1958. [14] pp. illus.

92 works (14 reproduced). *See also* bibl. 91.

1959

112 NEW YORK. FINE ARTS ASSOCIATES. *Picasso: The Bathers.* Feb. 10–Mar. 7, 1959. [6] pp. illus.

Includes excerpts from "Les baigneurs de Picasso," by Georges A. Salles (bibl. 50). Also shown at the Museum of Fine Arts, Boston, Mar. 15–Apr. 15, 1959.

1960

113 NEW YORK. SIDNEY JANIS GALLERY. *Picasso, 1881-   : His Blue Period (1900-1905). Collection of Pastels, Water-colours*

and Drawings. Also, the Complete Set of Small Bronzes of Female Figures 1945-47. Apr. 25–May 21, 1960. [60] pp. illus.
   68 works (24 sculptures, all reproduced). Also shown at the O'Hana Gallery, London; Stoneleigh Abbey, Warwickshire; and the Galerie Motte, Geneva, through Sept. 10, 1960.

114 FAENZA. MUSEO INTERNAZIONALE DELLE CERAMICHE. 42 ceramiche originali di Pablo Picasso. Aug. 1–Oct. 15, 1960. 12 pp. plus 26 pl.
   Introduction by Giuseppe Liverani.

1961-1962

115 DÜSSELDORF. KUNSTVEREIN. Pablo Picasso: Keramik aus der Manufaktur Madoura. Dec. 5, 1961–Jan. 21, 1962. 17 pp. illus.
   53 works (12 reproduced). Foreword by Karl-Heinz Hering. Introduction (in French and German) by André Verdet. Also includes "Zur Keramik von Pablo Picasso," by Georges Ramié.

1962

116 NEW YORK. OTTO GERSON GALLERY. "Sculpture," in Picasso: An American Tribute. John Richardson, ed. Apr. 25–May 12, 1962. New York: Public Education Association. [17] pp. illus.
   35 works (all reproduced). Section of catalogue of nine simultaneous exhibitions for the benefit of the Public Education Association.

1964

117 TORONTO. ART GALLERY. Picasso and Man. Jan. 11–Feb. 16, 1964. 160 pp. illus.
   276 works (8 sculptures, all reproduced, with commentaries). Includes "Picasso, the Early Years," by Jean Sutherland Boggs; "Picasso, the 'Demoiselles d'Avignon' and Cubism," by John Golding; "Picasso as a Surrealist," by Robert Rosenblum; "Picasso since 1937," by Evan H. Turner. Catalogue by Jean Sutherland Boggs. Chron., bibl. Exhibition also shown at the Montreal Museum of Fine Arts, Feb. 28–Mar. 31, 1964.

118 HAMBURG. MUSEUM FÜR KUNST UND GEWERBE. Pablo Picasso: Keramik 1947 bis 1961. Mosaiken 1956 bis 1958. Linolschnitte seit 1961. Lithographien 1956 bis 1961. Plakate 1948 bis 1962. Jan. 31–Mar. 22, 1964. [78] pp. illus.
   143 works (31 ceramics, 28 reproduced). Includes "Keramik," by Daniel-Henry Kahnweiler (excerpts from bibl. 70).

1966

119 WASHINGTON, D.C. GALLERY OF MODERN ART. Picasso since 1945. June 30–Sept. 4, 1966. 63 pp. illus.
   97 works (11 sculptures, all reproduced; 6 ceramics, 2 reproduced). Introduction by Eleanor Green.

120 VALLAURIS. GALERIE MADOURA. Picasso: 20 ans de céramiques chez Madoura. 1946-1966. July 1966. [41] pp. illus.
   120 works (16 reproduced). Introduction by Madoura [Georges and Suzanne Ramié].

121 PARIS. GALERIE JEANNE BUCHER. Picasso et le béton. Nov. 1966. [14] pp. illus.
   Photographs, scale models, and plans of sculpture in molded and sandblasted concrete by Carl Nesjar. Short essays by Pierre Gascar, Georges Patrix, Michel Ragon, and Daniel L. Gervis. See also bibl. 123, 125.

1966-1967

122 PARIS. PETIT PALAIS. "Dessins, sculptures, céramiques," in Hommage à Pablo Picasso. Nov. 1966–Feb. 1967. [241] pp. illus., bibl.
   508 works (187 sculptures, all reproduced, with some commentaries; 116 ceramics, all reproduced). One of three parts of 85th anniversary exhibition; paintings shown at Grand Palais, prints at Bibliothèque Nationale. Chron. in paintings catalogue.

1967

123 LONDON. INSTITUTE OF CONTEMPORARY ARTS GALLERY. Picasso and Concrete: New Techniques and Photographs by Carl Nesjar. Jan. 11–Feb. 11, 1967. [10] pp. illus.
   Exhibition similar to bibl. 121. Introduction by Pierre Gascar, translated by Joyce Reeves. Comments by Carl Nesjar. See also bibl. 125.

124 DALLAS. MUSEUM OF FINE ARTS. Picasso: Two Concurrent Retrospective Exhibitions. Feb. 8–Mar. 26, 1967. 104 pp. illus.
   312 works (8 sculptures, 1 reproduced). Shown concurrently at the Dallas Museum of Fine Arts (paintings, sculpture, and graphics) and the Fort Worth Art Center Museum (drawings, watercolors, and pastels). Introduction and text by Douglas Cooper. Chron., bibl.

125 ST. GALLEN. KUNSTMUSEUM. Picasso et le béton. Apr. 9–May 21, 1967. [20] pp. illus.
   Exhibition similar to bibl. 121, 123. Introduction by Pierre Gascar (in French and German). Text by Daniel Gervis.

126 LONDON. TATE GALLERY. Picasso: Sculpture, Ceramics, Graphic Work. June 9–Aug. 13, 1967. London: Arts Council of Great Britain. 132 pp. illus.
   275 works (203 sculptures, all reproduced, pp. 26-108; 31 ceramics, all reproduced, pp. 109-119). Introduction and commentaries by Roland Penrose. Chron., bibl.

All works are lent by the artist except where otherwise stated. The catalogue is divided into the following categories: Sculpture and Constructions, Ceramics, Drawings and Collages, and Prints, and is arranged chronologically within each section. Dates and locations, as well as dimensions of the sculpture, with certain modifications, are taken from the catalogue of the exhibition *Hommage à Pablo Picasso* (Paris, Petit Palais, winter 1966-1967). Further information has been supplied in the catalogue of the exhibition held June-August, 1967, at the Tate Gallery, London, organized by the Arts Council of Great Britain. Dates given to bronzes refer to the original in plaster or clay. On the drawings and prints, dates in parentheses do not appear on the works. Dimensions are given in inches and centimeters, height preceding length and depth.

SCULPTURE AND CONSTRUCTIONS

1 *Seated Woman*. Barcelona, 1901. Bronze, 5½ x 3⅛ x 2¾ inches (14 x 8 x 7 cm.). Signed "Picasso c." *Page 50*

2 *Mask of a Blind Singer*. Barcelona, 1903. Bronze, 5⅛ x 2¾ x 3⅛ inches (13 x 7 x 8 cm.). *Page 51*

3 *Mask of a Picador with a Broken Nose*. Barcelona, 1903? Bronze, 7¼ x 5⅛ x 4⅜ inches (18.5 x 13 x 11.2 cm.). Signed and dated "Picasso/04" and "04-1905"; cf. Zervos VI, no. 579. *Page 51*

4 *Alice Derain*. Paris, 1905. Bronze, 10⅝ x 10⅝ x 5½ inches (27 x 27 x 14 cm.). Signed "Picasso" and numbered "oo." *Page 53*

5 *Head of a Jester*. Paris, 1905. Bronze, 15 x 14⅜ x 8½ inches (38.2 x 36.5 x 21.6 cm.). Signed "Piccasso" (*sic*). Zervos I, no. 322. Collection Mrs. Bertram Smith, New York. *Page 52*

6 *Fernande*. Paris, 1905-1906. Bronze, 13⅜ x 9⅞ x 10½ inches (34 x 25 x 26.5 cm.). Signed "Picasso" and numbered "8/9." *Page 53*

7 *Kneeling Woman Combing Her Hair*. 1905-1906. Bronze, 16⅜ x 12¼ x 11½ inches (41.6 x 31.2 x 29.2 cm.). Signed "Picasso." The Baltimore Museum of Art, Cone Collection. *Page 49*

8 *Head of a Woman*. 1906. Bronze relief, 4⅞ x 2¼ inches (12.5 x 5.8 cm.). Joseph H. Hirshhorn Collection. *Page 54*

9 *Figure*. Paris, 1907. Carved wood, 32¼ x 9½ x 8½ inches (82 x 24 x 21.5 cm.). Zervos II², no. 607. *Page 55*

10 *Figurine*. Paris, 1907. Bronze, after carved wood, 8⅝ x 2⅜ x 2⅜ inches (22 x 6 x 6 cm.). *Page 55*

11 *Mask of a Woman*. Paris, 1908. Bronze, 7½ x 6¼ inches (19 x 16 cm.). Signed and dated "Picasso 1908." Collection Mr. and Mrs. Sampson R. Field, New York. *Page 54*

12 *Seated Woman*. 1908. Bronze, 4 inches (10 cm.) high. Collection Mr. and Mrs. Alan H. Cummings, Winnetka, Illinois. *Page 57*

13 *Woman's Head*. Paris, 1909. Bronze, 16¼ x 10⅜ x 10¾ inches (41.3 x 26.2 x 27.2 cm.). Signed "Picasso." Zervos II², no. 573. The Museum of Modern Art, New York, purchase. *Page 56*

14 *Guitar*. Paris, 1912. Sheet metal and wire, 30¾ x 13¾ x 7¼ inches (78 x 35 x 18.5 cm.). Zervos II¹, no. 773. *Page 58*

15 *Violin*. Paris, 1913. Pasted paper, chalk and gouache on cardboard, 20 x 11¾ inches (51 x 30 cm.). Zervos II², no. 784. *Page 59*

16 *Violin*. Paris, 1913-1914. Cardboard and string, 23 x 8¼ x 3 inches (58.5 x 21 x 7.5 cm.). *Page 58*

17 *Glass and Dice*. Paris, 1914. Painted wood, 9¼ x 8⅝ inches (23.5 x 22 cm.). Zervos II², no. 839. *Page 63*

18 *Glass of Absinth*. Paris, 1914. Painted bronze with silver spoon, 8½ inches (21.6 cm.) high. Zervos II², no. 584. The Museum of Modern Art, New York, gift of Mrs. Bertram Smith. *Frontispiece*

19 *Glass, Pipe, and Playing Card*. Paris, 1914. Painted wood and metal, 13⅜ inches (34 cm.) diameter. Zervos II², no. 830. *Page 60*

20 *Guitar*. 1914. Painted metal, 37⅜ x 26 x 7½ inches (95 x 66 x 19 cm.). Zervos II², no. 580. *Page 61*

21 *Musical Instruments*. Paris, 1914. Painted wood, 23⅝ x 14⅛ x 8⅝ inches (60 x 36 x 22 cm.). Zervos II², no. 853. *Page 63*

22 *Still Life*. 1914. Painted wood with upholstery fringe, 10 x 18⅞ x 4 inches (25.5 x 48 x 10 cm.). Collection Lady Penrose, London. *Page 62*

23 *Violin and Bottle on a Table*. Paris, 1915-1916. Painted wood, tacks, and string, 18½ x 16½ x 7½ inches (47 x 42 x 19 cm.). Zervos II², no. 926. *Page 63*

24 *Packet of Tobacco*. Paris, 1921. Painted metal, 6⅝ x 18⅞ inches (17 x 48 cm.). *Page 64*

25 *Guitar*. 1924. Painted metal, 42½ x 24⅜ x 9⅞ inches (108 x 62 x 25 cm.). Zervos V, no. 217. *Page 64*

26 *Construction in Wire*. 1928-1929. Iron wire, 19⅝ x 16⅛ x 6¾ inches (50 x 41 x 17 cm.). *Page 65*

27 *Woman in the Garden*. 1929-1930. Bronze, after welded iron, 82¾ x 46 x 32¼ inches (210 x 117 x 82 cm.). *Page 67*

28 *Construction with Glove (By the Sea)*. Juan-les-Pins, 1930. Cardboard, plaster and wood on canvas, covered with sand, 10⅝ x 14 inches (27 x 35.5 cm.). *Page 72*

29 *Woman*. 1930-1932. Welded iron, 31⅞ x 9⅞ x 12⅝ inches (81 x 25 x 32 cm.). *Page 66*

79 *Cat.* Paris, 1944. Bronze, 14⅛ x 21⅝ x 6⅞ inches (36 x 55 x 17.5 cm.). *Page 97*

80 *Death's Head (Flayed Head).* Paris, 1944. Bronze, 11⅜ x 8⅜ x 10¼ inches (29 x 21.3 x 26 cm.). *Page 108*

81 *Figure.* Paris, 1944. Bronze, 60½ x 22 x 7½ inches (153.7 x 56 x 19 cm.), on stone base. *Page 99*

82 *Man with Sheep.* Paris, 1944. Bronze, 86½ x 30¾ x 28⅜ inches (220 x 78 x 72 cm.). *Pages 106, 107*

83 *Woman.* 1945. Bronze, 10 inches (25.4 cm.) high. Numbered "1/10." Collection Mrs. G. David Thompson, Pittsburgh. *Page 110, right*

84 *Woman.* 1945. Bronze, 9⅛ inches (23.2 cm.) high. Numbered "2/10." Collection Mrs. G. David Thompson, Pittsburgh. *Page 111, left*

85 *Woman.* 1945. Bronze, 9½ inches (24 cm.) high. Numbered "5/10." Collection Mrs. G. David Thompson, Pittsburgh. *Page 111, right*

86 *Woman.* 1945. Bronze, 8⅞ inches (22.4 cm.) high. Numbered "1/10." Collection Mrs. G. David Thompson, Pittsburgh. *Page 110, left*

87 *Woman.* 1945. Bronze, 5¼ inches (13.3 cm.) high. Numbered "1/10." Collection Mrs. G. David Thompson, Pittsburgh. *Page 112, left*

88 *Torso of a Woman.* 1946. Bronze, 11 inches (28 cm.) high, on wood base. *Page 113*

89 *Seated Woman.* 1947. Bronze, 4¾ inches (12 cm.) high. Numbered "1/10." Collection Mrs. G. David Thompson, Pittsburgh. *Page 112, right*

90 *Woman.* 1947. Bronze, 7⅝ inches (19.4 cm.) high. Numbered "1/10." Collection Mrs. G. David Thompson, Pittsburgh. *Page 113*

91 *Woman.* 1947. Bronze, 7¾ inches (19.5 cm.) high. Numbered "1/10." Collection Mrs. G. David Thompson, Pittsburgh. *Page 114*

92 *Hand with Sleeve.* 1947. Bronze, 2¾ x 9 x 4⅜ inches (7 x 23 x 11 cm.). Collection Mary and Sylvan Lang, San Antonio, Texas. *Page 116*

93 *Vase-Face.* Vallauris, 1947. Bronze, 11 x 4 x 5½ inches (28 x 10 x 14 cm.). *Page 115*

94 *Animal Head.* Vallauris, 1948. Bronze, 14⅛ x 9½ x 8¼ inches (36 x 24 x 21 cm.). *Page 118*

95 *Centaur.* Vallauris, 1948. Bronze, 15½ x 11¾ x 6¼ inches (39.4 x 30 x 16 cm.). Dated "8.1.48." *Page 119*

96 *Vase-Woman.* Vallauris, 1948. Bronze, 37¾ x 10¼ x 7⅞ inches (96 x 26 x 20 cm.). *Page 114*

97 *Female Form.* Vallauris, 1948? Bronze, 50 x 14½ x 4 inches (127 x 37 x 10 cm.). *Page 117*

98 *Glass.* Vallauris, 1949. Bronze, 8⅝ x 4¾ x 8⅝ inches (22 x 12 x 22 cm.). *Page 119*

99 *Mask of a Faun.* Vallauris, 1949-1950. Bronze, 15¾ x 10⅝ inches (40 x 27 cm.). *Page 118*

100 *Hand.* Vallauris, 1950. Bronze, 1¾ x 7⅞ inches (4.5 x 20 cm.). *Page 124*

101 *Little Girl Skipping Rope.* Vallauris, 1950. Bronze, after found objects, 60¼ x 25⅝ x 24⅜ inches (153 x 65 x 62 cm.). *Page 128*

102 *Mask of a Woman.* Vallauris, 1950. Bronze, 10½ x 11¼ x 6⅞ inches (26.5 x 28.5 x 17.5 cm.). Inscribed and dated "Vallauris 20.7.50." *Page 124*

103 *Owl.* Vallauris, 1950. Bronze, 13 x 12⅝ x 13⅜ inches (33 x 32 x 34 cm.). *Page 127, above*

104 *Owl.* Vallauris, 1950. Bronze, 14½ x 10¼ x 10¼ inches (37 x 26 x 26 cm.). *Page 127, below*

105 *Pregnant Woman.* Vallauris, 1950. Bronze, first version, 41¼ inches (104.8 cm.) high. Numbered "2/6." The Museum of Modern Art, New York, gift of Mrs. Bertram Smith. *Page 125*

106 *She-Goat.* Vallauris, 1950. Bronze, after found objects, 46⅜ x 56⅜ x 27¾ inches (118 x 143.2 x 70.5 cm.). The Museum of Modern Art, New York, Mrs. Simon Guggenheim Fund. *Page 126*

107 *Woman with Baby Carriage.* Vallauris, 1950. Bronze, after found objects, 80 x 23⅝ x 57 inches (203 x 60 x 145 cm.). *Page 129*

108 *Baboon and Young.* Vallauris, 1951. Bronze, after found objects, 21 x 13¼ x 20¾ inches (53.4 x 33.2 x 52.7 cm.). Dated "1951" and numbered "5/6." The Museum of Modern Art, New York, Mrs. Simon Guggenheim Fund. *Page 134*

109 *Head of a Woman.* Vallauris, 1951. Bronze, 21⅛ x 7⅜ x 14⅛ inches (53.6 x 18.8 x 35.7 cm.). Numbered "2/6." The Museum of Modern Art, New York, Benjamin Scharps and David Scharps Fund. *Page 130*

110 *Head of a Woman.* Vallauris, 1951. Bronze, 19⅞ x 8⅝ x 14½ inches (50.5 x 22 x 37 cm.). *Page 131*

111 *Goat Skull and Bottle.* Vallauris, 1951-1952. Painted bronze, after found objects, 31 x 37⅝ x 21½ inches (78.8 x 95.6 x 54.5 cm.). The Museum of Modern Art, New York, Mrs. Simon Guggenheim Fund. *Page 132*

112 *Crane.* Vallauris, 1952. Painted bronze, after found objects, 29½ x 11½ x 17 inches (75 x 29 x 43 cm.). *Page 133*

113 *Woman Reading.* Vallauris, 1952-1953. Painted bronze, after found objects, 6⅛ x 14 x 5⅛ inches (15.6 x 35.3 x 12.9 cm.). Collection Mr. and Mrs. Gerald Gidwitz, Highland Park, Illinois. *Page 135*

114 *Angry Owl.* Vallauris, 1953. Bronze, after found objects, 10⅝ x 8⅝ x 11 inches (27 x 22 x 28 cm.). *Page 135*

115 *Bunch of Flowers.* Vallauris, 1953. Bronze, 23⅝ x 19⅝ x 15⅜ inches (60 x 50 x 39 cm.). *Page 137*

116 *Flowers in a Vase.* Vallauris, 1953. Bronze, 28¾ x 19¼ x 16½ inches (73 x 49 x 42 cm.). *Page 136*

117 *Vase with Flower.* Vallauris, 1953. Bronze, 29 x 17¼ x 6 inches (74 x 44 x 15 cm.). *Page 137*

118 *Woman.* Vallauris, 1953. Painted wood, 54 x 17¾ x 6⅞ (137 x 45 x 17.5 cm.). *Page 146, left*

119 *Dove.* Vallauris, 1953. Bronze, 6¾ x 11 x 4¾ inches (17 x 28 x 12 cm.). Dated "29.1.53." *Page 145, center*

120 *Dove.* Vallauris, 1953. Bronze, 5½ x 9 x 4⅜ inches (14 x 23 x 11 cm.). Dated "14.10.53." *Page 145, above*

121 *Woman.* Vallauris, 1953. Painted wood, 35½ x 7¼ x 2½ inches (90 x 18.5 x 6.5 cm.). *Page 146, right*

122 *Woman.* Vallauris, 1953. Bronze, 20½ x 4 x 4¾ inches (52 x 10 x 12 cm.). Dated "6.1.53." *Page 144*

123 *Woman Carrying a Child.* Vallauris, 1953. Painted wood, 69 x 20½ x 13 inches (175 x 52 x 33 cm.). *Page 147*

124 *Bust of Sylvette.* Vallauris, 1954. Metal cutout, folded and painted, 27½ x 17¼ inches (70 x 44 cm.). *Page 148*

125 *Bust of Sylvette.* Vallauris, 1954. Metal cutout, folded and painted, 27⅛ x 17⅜ inches (69 x 44.2 cm.). *Page 149*

126 *Bust of Sylvette.* Vallauris, 1954. Metal cutout, folded and painted, 24⅜ x 17⅜ inches (62 x 44.2 cm.). *Page 150*

127 *Bust of Sylvette.* Vallauris, 1954. Metal cutout, folded and painted, 23¼ x 13 inches (59 x 33 cm.). *Page 151*

128 *Head of a Woman.* Vallauris, 1954. Metal cutout, painted, 34¼ x 10¾ x 10¾ inches (87 x 27.5 x 27.5 cm.). *Page 153*

129 *Head of a Woman.* Vallauris, 1954. Metal cutout, painted, 32 x 13½ x 12¾ inches (81 x 34.5 x 32.5 cm.). *Page 152*

130 *Head of a Woman.* Vallauris, 1954. Wood cutout, painted, 31½ x 11 x 13¾ inches (80 x 28 x 35 cm.). *Page 154*

131 *Head of a Woman.* Vallauris, 1954. Metal cutout, painted, 30¼ x 10⅜ x 14¼ inches (77 x 26.5 x 36 cm.). *Page 155*

132 *Young Man.* 1956. Bronze, after wood, 31½ x 16⅛ x 9 inches (80 x 41 x 23 cm.). *Page 157*

133 *Bull.* 1957. Bronze, 15¾ x 26 x 8½ inches (40 x 66 x 21.5 cm.). *Page 158*

134 *Bull.* 1957. Bronze, 6½ inches (16.5 cm.) long. Collection Larry Aldrich, New York. *Page 160, right*

135 *Bull's Head.* 1957. Bronze, 14½ x 7⅞ x 7⅛ inches (37 x 20 x 18 cm.). *Page 158*

136 *Head of a Woman with Necklace.* 1957. Bronze, 14¼ x 3½ x 5½ inches (36 x 9 x 14 cm.). *Page 161*

137 *Pigeon.* 1957. Bronze, 6 x 9⅞ x 4¼ inches (15 x 25 x 11 cm.). *Page 161*

138 *Little Girl.* 1957-1958. Painted bronze, 17 x 4½ x 8¾ inches (43 x 11.5 x 22.3 cm.). *Page 162*

139 *Bather Playing.* 1958. Bronze, after found objects, 44½ x 13 x 25 inches (113 x 33 x 63.5 cm.). *Page 165*

140 *Bull.* 1958. Bronze, 4¾ inches (12.1 cm.) long. Collection Mr. and Mrs. Victor W. Ganz, New York. *Page 160, left*

141 *Figure.* 1958. Wood, 53⅛ x 9½ inches (135 x 24 cm.). *Page 163*

142 *Head.* Cannes, 1958. Bronze, after wood, 20 x 8½ x 6⅛ inches (51 x 21.5 x 15.5 cm.). *Page 166*

143 *Man.* 1958. Wood, 46¾ x 29½ x 11¾ inches (119 x 75 x 30 cm.). *Page 164*

144 *Man.* 1958. Bronze, after wood, 22½ x 5⅛ x 5½ inches (57 x 13 x 14 cm.). Dated "20.7.58." *Page 167*

145 *Head of a Woman with Blonde Hair.* 1958-1959. Wood and wicker basket, 32¼ x 21¼ x 2⅜ inches (82 x 54 x 6 cm.). *Page 168*

146 *Arm.* 1959. Bronze, 22¾ inches (57.8 cm.) high. Signed "Picasso" and dated "15.3.59." Joseph H. Hirshhorn Collection. *Page 159*

147 *Figure.* Cannes, 1960. Bronze, after wood and found objects, 48⅜ x 18½ x 7⅛ inches (123 x 47 x 18 cm.). *Page 170*

148 *Head of a Woman.* Cannes, 1960. Metal cutout, folded and painted, 13¾ x 9⅞ inches (35 x 25 cm.). *Page 203*

149 *Man Running.* Cannes, 1960. Bronze, 46 x 25⅛ x 3⅛ inches (117 x 64 x 8 cm.). *Page 172*

150 *Man with Javelin.* Cannes, 1960. Bronze, after wood, 45⅝ x 13¾ x 33⅞ inches (116 x 35 x 86 cm.). *Page 171*

151 *Sparrow Hawk.* Cannes, 1960. Metal cutout, 11⅜ x 5½ x 3⅛ inches (29 x 14 x 8 cm.). *Page 182*

152 *Bather.* Cannes, 1961. Metal cutout, folded and painted, 20⅛ x 6⅞ x 8¼ inches (51 x 17.5 x 21 cm.). *Page 184*

153 *Bird.* Cannes, 1961. Metal cutout, folded and painted, 15 x 16⅛ inches (38 x 41 cm.). *Page 183*

154 *Bust of a Woman.* Cannes, 1961. Metal cutout, folded and painted, 12⅞ x 6½ inches (32.7 x 16.5 cm.). *Page 178*

155 *Chair.* Cannes, 1961. Metal cutout, folded and painted, 43¾ x 29⅛ x 23⅝ inches (111 x 74 x 60 cm.). *Page 175*

156 *Clown.* Cannes, 1961. Metal cutout, folded and painted, 12¼ x 10⅝ x 4¾ inches (31 x 27 x 12 cm.). *Page 194*

157 *Cock.* Cannes, 1961. Metal cutout, folded and painted, 8⅝ x 10⅝ x 3 inches (22 x 27 x 7.5 cm.). *Page 183*

158 *Football Player.* Cannes, 1961. Metal cutout, folded and painted, 22½ x 18⅞ inches (57 x 48 cm.). *Page 194, left*

159 *Football Player.* Cannes, 1961. Metal cutout, folded and painted, 23¼ x 19¼ inches (59 x 49 cm.). *Page 194, right*

160 *Head.* Cannes, 1961. Metal cutout, folded and painted, 6⅝ x 5½ inches (17 x 14 cm.). *Page 194*

161 *Head.* Cannes, 1961. Metal cutout, folded and painted, 12⅛ x 2 x 2¾ inches (31 x 5 x 7 cm.). *Page 179*

162 *Head of a Bearded Man.* Cannes, 1961. Metal cutout, folded and painted, 15 x 9⅝ x 3⅜ inches (38 x 24.5 x 8.5 cm.). *Page 190, below*

163 *Head of a Bearded Man.* Cannes, 1961. Metal cutout, folded and painted, 16⅛ x 11¾ inches (41 x 30 cm.). *Page 190, above*

164 *Head of a Bearded Man.* Cannes, 1961. Metal cutout, folded and painted, 31½ x 24⅜ inches (80 x 62 cm.). *Page 189*

165 *Head of a Man.* Cannes, 1961. Metal cutout, folded and painted, 11 x 7½ inches (28 x 19 cm.). *Page 191*

166 *Head of a Woman.* Cannes, 1961. Metal cutout, folded and painted, 8⅝ x 6¾ x 3⅛ inches (22 x 17 x 8 cm.). *Page 191, below left*

167 *Head of a Woman*. Cannes, 1961. Bronze, 10⅝ x 5⅞ x 9 inches (27 x 15 x 23 cm.). Dated "19.2.61." *Page 173*

168 *Head of a Woman*. Cannes, 1961. Metal cutout, folded and painted, 11 x 7⅞ x 1¼ inches (28 x 20 x 3 cm.). *Page 191, below right*

169 *Head of a Woman*. Cannes, 1961. Metal cutout, folded and painted, 15 x 11¾ inches (38 x 30 cm.). *Page 191, above right*

170 *Head of a Woman*. Cannes, 1961. Metal cutout, folded and painted, 31½ x 21⅝ inches (80 x 55 cm.). *Page 188*

171 *Little Monkey*. Cannes, 1961. Metal cutout, folded and painted, 6¾ x 4½ inches (17 x 11.5 cm.). *Page 178*

172 *Man with Sheep*. Cannes, 1961. Metal cutout, folded and painted, 17¼ x 13¾ inches (44 x 35 cm.). *Page 181*

173 *Man with Sheep*. Cannes, 1961. Metal cutout, folded and painted, 20⅞ x 11 inches (53 x 28 cm.). *Page 180*

174 *Man with Staff*. Cannes, 1961. Bronze, 15 x 9½ x 8¼ inches (38 x 24 x 21 cm.). *Page 173*

175 *Musician*. Cannes, 1961. Bronze, 17¾ x 4¾ x 6¼ inches (45 x 12 x 16 cm.). *Page 173*

176 *Owl*. Cannes, 1961. Metal cutout, folded and painted, 9⅞ x 9⅝ inches (25 x 24.5 cm.). *Page 183*

177 *Owl*. Cannes, 1961. Metal cutout, folded and painted, 15 x 7⅛ inches (38 x 18 cm.). *Page 182, left*

178 *Owl*. Cannes, 1961. Metal cutout, folded and painted, 16⅛ x 6⅝ inches (41 x 17 cm.). *Page 182, right*

179 *Pierrot*. Cannes, 1961. Metal cutout, folded and painted, 53⅛ x 20½ x 18⅞ inches (135 x 52 x 48 cm.). *Page 185*

180 *Small Woman with Outstretched Arms*. Cannes, 1961. Metal cutout, folded and painted, 14½ x 14½ x 2 inches (37 x 37 x 5 cm.). *Page 192, below*

181 *The Spanish Woman*. Cannes, 1961. Metal cutout, folded and painted, 11 x 5⅞ inches (28 x 15 cm.). *Page 187*

182 *The Spanish Woman*. Cannes, 1961. Metal cutout, folded and painted, 8¼ x 5⅞ (21 x 15 cm.). *Page 186, right*

183 *The Spanish Woman*. Cannes, 1961. Metal cutout, folded and painted, 11 x 5⅞ inches (28 x 15 cm.). *Page 187*

184 *Woman*. Cannes, 1961. Metal cutout, folded and painted, 17 x 8⅝ (43.2 x 22 cm.). *Page 184*

185 *Woman and Child*. Cannes, 1961. Metal cutout, folded and painted, 17¼ x 6⅞ inches (44 x 17.5 cm.). *Page 174, left*

186 *Woman and Child*. Cannes, 1961. Metal cutout, folded and painted, 17¼ x 6⅞ inches (44 x 17.5 cm.). *Page 174, right*

187 *Woman and Child*. Cannes, 1961. Metal cutout, folded and painted, 50¾ x 21⅝ inches (129 x 55 cm.). *Page 176*

188 *Woman with Bowl*. Cannes, 1961. Metal cutout, folded and painted, 44⅞ x 25¼ inches (114 x 64 cm.). *Page 177*

189 *Woman with Open Arms*. Cannes, 1961. Metal cutout, folded and painted, 11 x 7½ inches (28 x 19 cm.). *Page 192, above*

190 *Woman with Outstretched Arms*. Cannes, 1961. Metal cutout, folded and painted, 72 x 67¾ x 31½ inches (183 x 172 x 80 cm.). *Page 193*

191 *Woman with Raised Arm*. Cannes, 1961. Metal cutout, folded and painted, 13⅜ x 4 inches (34 x 10 cm.). *Page 179*

192 *Bust of a Woman*. Mougins, 1962. Metal cutout, folded and painted, 17¾ x 14¼ inches (45 x 36 cm.). *Page 202*

193 *Head of a Woman*. Mougins, 1962. Metal cutout, folded and painted, 9⅞ x 7⅛ inches (25 x 18 cm.). *Page 195*

194 *Head of a Woman*. Mougins, 1962. Metal cutout, folded and painted, 12⅝ x 7⅞ inches (32 x 20 cm.). *Page 201*

195 *Head of a Woman*. Mougins, 1962. Metal cutout, folded and painted, 12⅝ x 10 inches (32 x 25.5 cm.). *Page 169*

196 *Head of a Woman*. Mougins, 1962. Metal cutout, folded and painted, 19⅝ x 11¾ inches (50 x 30 cm.). *Page 199*

197 *Head of a Woman*. Mougins, 1962. Metal cutout, folded and painted, 19⅝ x 11¾ inches (50 x 30 cm.). *Page 200*

198 *Head of a Woman*. Mougins, 1962. Metal cutout, folded and painted, 19⅝ x 15¾ inches (50 x 40 cm.). *Page 204*

199 *Head of a Woman*. Mougins, 1962. Metal cutout, folded and painted, 19⅝ x 19⅝ x 11¾ inches (50 x 50 x 30 cm.). *Page 205*

200 *Head of a Woman*. Mougins, 1962. Metal cutout, folded, 20½ x 10⅞ x 7 inches (52 x 27.7 x 18 cm.). *Page 206*

201 *Jacqueline with a Green Ribbon*. Mougins, 1962. Metal cutout, folded and painted, 20½ x 11½ inches (52 x 29 cm.). *Page 198*

202 *Man with Moustache*. Mougins, 1962. Metal cutout, folded and painted, 11¾ x 17 inches (30 x 43 cm.). *Page 195*

203 *Woman*. Mougins, 1962. Bronze, 12¾ x 6¾ x 20⅛ inches (32.5 x 17 x 51 cm.). *Page 173*

204 Model for the Chicago Civic Center sculpture. 1965. Welded steel, 41¼ x 27½ x 19 inches (104.8 x 70 x 48 cm.). The Art Institute of Chicago, gift of Pablo Picasso. *Page 207*

CERAMIC SCULPTURE
(All made in Vallauris, 1948-1963)

205 *Seated Bird*. 1948. Modeled from clay slabs; slip-painted; heightened with enamel (polychrome on white body). 9¼ x 4¼ x 15⅜ inches (23.5 x 11 x 39 cm.). Dated "4.2.48." *Page 120*

206 *Woman (Femme drapée)*. 1948. Wheel-thrown and modeled; slip-painted. 14⅞ inches (37.8 cm.) high. Galerie Chalette, New York. *Page 121*

207 *Condor*. 1949. Wheel-thrown and modeled; slip-painted and partly glazed. 17 x 15¾ x 8¼ inches (43.2 x 40 x 21 cm.). *Page 120*

208 *Owl*. 1949. Wheel-thrown and modeled; incised and slip-painted. 7⅞ x 8¼ x 5¼ inches (19.7 x 21 x 13.4 cm.). Dated underneath "30.12.49." *Page 120*

209 *Woman with Hands Hidden*. 1949. Wheel-thrown and modeled; slip-painted. 18½ x 5⅞ x 3½ inches (47 x 15 x 9 cm.). *Page 122*

210 *Woman with Mantilla*. 1949. Wheel-thrown and modeled; slip-painted. 18½ x 4½ x 2¾ inches (47 x 1.5 x 7 cm.). *Page 122*

211 *Centaur.* 1950. Wheel-thrown parts; wax-resist decoration. 17 x 9⅞ x 5½ inches. (43.2 x 25 x 14 cm.). *Page 123*

212 *Large Sculptured Head.* 1950. Wheel-thrown and modeled; incised, slip-painted, and glazed; heightened with white enamel. 15 x 9⅞ x 11¾ inches (38 x 25.1 x 29.8 cm.). *Page 123*

213 *Large Sculptured Head with a Bow.* 1950. Wheel-thrown and modeled; incised, slip-painted, and glazed; heightened with white enamel. 14½ x 9½ x 11¾ inches (37 x 24.2 x 30 cm.). *Page 123*

214 *Two-handled Pitcher.* 1950. Incised, slip-painted, and partly glazed. 13 x 11 inches (33 x 28 cm.). Dated "2.1.50 II." *Page 123*

215 *Owl.* 1951. Slip-painted, unglazed. 13⅜ x 13¾ x 8⅝ inches (34 x 35 x 22 cm.). Signed and dated "Picasso 11.11.51." *Page 140, below*

216 *Dove.* 1953. Modeled from a clay slab; slip-painted, 4¾ x 8⅝ x 5⅛ inches (12 x 22 x 13 cm.). *Page 143*

217 *Dove.* 1953. Modeled from clay slabs; slip-painted. 5½ x 7⅞ x 3¼ inches (14 x 19.7 x 8.3 cm.). Dated "7.1.53." *Page 142, above, left*

218 *Dove.* 1953. Modeled from a clay slab; slip-painted, unglazed. 5⅞ x 9⅞ x 5⅛ inches (15 x 25 x 13 cm.). *Page 142, below, right*

219 *Dove.* 1953. Modeled from a clay slab; slip-painted, unglazed. 5⅞ x 10¼ x 5⅛ inches (15 x 26 x 13 cm.). *Page 142, below, left*

220 *Dove with Eggs.* 1953. Modeled from clay slabs; slip-painted. 5½ x 8⅝ x 7⅞ inches (14 x 22 x 20 cm.). Inscribed "29.1.53." *Page 142*

221 *Kneeling Woman.* 1953. Wheel-thrown and modeled; painted in oxides on tin glaze. 11⅜ x 6⅜ x 5⅞ inches (29 x 16.2 x 15 cm.). *Page 138*

222 *Little Bull.* 1953. Cut out and modeled from a slab of white clay. 3½ x 9⅞ x 5⅛ inches (9 x 25 x 13 cm.). *Page 145*

223 *Owl.* 1953. Slip-painted, unglazed. 13⅝ x 10¼ x 13 inches (34.7 x 26 x 33 cm.). Signed "Picasso" and inscribed underneath "5.1.53 Vallauris." *Page 140, above*

224 *Owl with Man's Face (Carnaval).* 1953. Slip-painted, unglazed. 13¾ x 13¾ x 11 inches (35 x 35 x 28 cm.). Inscribed "Carnaval" and dated underneath "27.2.53." *Page 141*

225 *Owl with Raised Wings.* 1953. Slip-painted, unglazed. 12¼ x 13 x 12¼ inches (31 x 33 x 31 cm.). Signed and dated "Picasso 6.2.53." *Page 141*

226 *Woman.* 1953. Wheel-thrown and modeled; slip-painted, heightened with enamel. 11⅜ x 2¾ x 2¾ inches (29 x 7 x 7 cm.). *Page 139*

227 *Woman.* 1953. Wheel-thrown and modeled; slip-painted, unglazed. 15⅜ x 4⅛ x 2⅛ inches (39 x 10.5 x 5.4 cm.). *Page 138*

228 *Woman in a Long Dress, Her Hair Undone.* 1953. Wheel-thrown and modeled; slip-painted and glazed. 11¾ inches (30 cm.) high, base 5⅞ x 9 inches (15 x 23 cm.). *Page 139*

229 *Woman with a Crown of Flowers.* 1954. Wheel-thrown and modeled; polychrome slip-painted decoration, glazed. 9½ x 7⅞ inches (24.2 x 20 cm.). Dated "20.3.54" and inscribed underneath "Pour Madame Ramié/Picasso." Collection M. and Mme Georges Ramié, Vallauris (A/M), France. *Page 143*

230 *Two-handled Vase (Great Bird).* 1961. Wheel-thrown; incised and slip-painted. 23¼ x 16⅛ x 17¼ inches (59 x 41 x 43.8 cm.). Dated "14.2.61." *Page 143*

231 *Face of a Woman.* 1962. Fragment of hollow brick, slip-painted and glazed. 8⅝ x 5⅛ x 3¾ inches (22 x 13 x 9.5 cm.). Dated "12.7.62." *Page 196, below, left*

232 *Face of a Woman.* 1962. Fragment of hollow brick, slip-painted, unglazed. 8⅝ x 6¼ x 3⅛ inches (22 x 16 x 8 cm.). Dated "12.7.62." *Page 196, above, left*

233 *Face of a Woman.* 1962. Fragment of hollow brick, slip-painted, unglazed. 8⅝ x 4¾ x 3⅛ inches (22 x 12 x 8 cm.). Dated "12.7.62." *Page 196, below, right*

234 *Face of a Bearded Man.* 1962. Fragment of hollow brick, slip-painted, unglazed. 8⅝ x 4⅞ x 3⅜ inches (22 x 12 x 8.6 cm.). Dated "17.7.62." *Page 196*

235 *Face.* 1963. Roman tile, slip-painted, partly glazed. 8⅝ x 19 inches (22 x 48.3 cm.). Dated "31.7.63." *Page 197, left*

236 *Face.* 1963. Roman tile, slip-painted, partly glazed. 19⅞ x 8⅝ inches. (50.5 x 22 cm.). Dated "31.7.63." *Page 197, right*

DRAWINGS AND COLLAGES

237 *Girl Combing Her Hair.* (Paris, 1905). Crayon, 22 x 16 inches (56 x 40.7 cm.). Zervos I, no. 341. Collection Sir Robert and Lady Sainsbury, London. *Page 211*

238 *Figure in Profile.* (1907). Pastel and watercolor, 24¾ x 18⅞ inches (63 x 48 cm.). *Page 211*

239 *Head.* (Paris, 1909). Gouache, 24 x 18 inches (61 x 45.7 cm.). Zervos II¹, no. 148. The Museum of Modern Art, New York, gift of Mrs. Saidie A. May

240 *Head of a Woman.* (Horta de Ebro, 1909). Conté crayon, 24¾ x 19 inches (63 x 48.3 cm.). cf. Zervos II¹, no. 162. *Page 211*

241 *Study for a Construction.* (Paris, 1912). Pen and ink, 6¾ x 4⅞ inches (17.2 x 12.4 cm.). Zervos II¹, no. 296. The Museum of Modern Art New York, purchase

242 *Glass and Dice.* (Paris, 1914). Pasted paper and charcoal, 9½ x 6¾ inches (24.2 x 17.2 cm.). Zervos II², no. 501. Heinz Berggruen, Paris. *Page 211*

243 *Pipe, Glass, Bottle of Rum.* Paris, 1914. Pasted paper, pencil, gouache, on cardboard, 15¾ x 20¾ inches (40 x 52.7 cm.). The Museum of Modern Art, New York, gift of Mr. and Mrs. Daniel Saidenberg

244 *Still Life with a Calling Card (Dice and Packet of Tobacco).* Paris, 1914. Pasted paper and crayon, 5½ x 8¼ inches (14 x 21 cm.). Zervos II², no. 490. Collection Mrs. Gilbert W. Chapman, New York

245 *Crucifixion.* Boisgeloup, 1932. Pen and ink, 13⅝ x 20⅛ inches (34.6 x 51.2 cm.). *Page 213*

246 *Crucifixion.* Boisgeloup, 1932. Pen and ink, 13½ x 20¾ inches (34.3 x 52.7 cm.)

247 *Head of a Woman (Design for Sculpture).* (1932). Charcoal on canvas, 36¼ x 28¾ inches (92 x 73 cm.). Galerie Beyeler, Basel. *Page 213*

248 Study for *Man with Sheep.* 1942. Pen and ink, 25⅝ x 19¾ inches (65.1 x 50.2 cm.). Zervos XII, no. 137

249 Study for *Man with Sheep.* 1943. Pen and ink, 26 x 20 inches (66 x 50.8 cm.). Zervos XII, no. 297

250 *Child's Head.* 1943. Pen and ink, 26 x 20 inches (66 x 50.8 cm.). Zervos XII, no. 301

251 Study for *Man with Sheep.* 1943. Pen and ink, 51⅛ x 20 inches (130 x 50.8 cm.). Zervos XII, no. 241. *Page 214*

252 *Head of a Woman (Study for Sculpture).* 1962. Pencil, 16½ x 10⅝ inches (42 x 27 cm.). Galerie Louise Leiris, Paris. *Page 214*

PRINTS

The following prints, from the so-called "Vollard Suite," are untitled but are categorized thematically. All are in the collection of The Museum of Modern Art; they are etchings, unless otherwise noted, and were acquired with the Abby Aldrich Rockefeller Fund.

Reference marks:

B. Fox, Milton S., ed. *Picasso for Vollard.* Introduction by Hans Bolliger. New York: Harry N. Abrams, Inc. (1956)

G. Geiser, Bernhard. *Picasso Peintre-Graveur.* Catalogue illustré de l'oeuvre gravé et lithographié 1899-1931. Berne: chez l'auteur, 1933

M. Mourlot, Fernand. *Picasso Lithographe.* Monte-Carlo: André Sauret (1949)

The Sculptor's Studio

253 (*ca.* March 1933). 10½ x 7⅝ inches (26.7 x 19.4 cm.). B.37

254 (*ca.* March 1933). 10½ x 7⅝ inches (26.7 x 19.4 cm.). B.39

255 March 21, 1933 10½ x 7⅝ inches (26.7 x 19.4 cm.). B.42

256 March 21, 1933. 10½ x 7⅝ inches (26.7 x 19.4 cm.). B.43

257 March 21, 1933. 10½ x 7⅝ inches (26.7 x 19.4 cm.). B.44. *Page 11*

258 March 25, 1933. 10½ x 7⅝ inches (26.7 x 19.4 cm.). B.46

259 March 26, 1933. 10½ x 7⅝ inches (26.7 x 19.4 cm.). B.48

260 March 26, 1933. 10½ x 7⅝ inches (26.7 x 19.4 cm.). B.49. *Page 9*

261 March 27, 1933. 10½ x 7⅝ inches (26.7 x 19.4 cm.). B.50

262 March 27, 1933. 10½ x 7⅝ inches (26.7 x 19.4 cm.). B.51

263 March 30, 1933. 7⅝ x 10½ inches (19.4 x 26.7 cm.). B.53

264 March 30, 1933. 7⅝ x 10½ inches (19.4 x 26.7 cm.). B.54

265 March 30, 1933. 7⅝ x 10½ inches (19.4 x 26.7 cm.). B.55

266 March 30, 1933. 7⅝ x 10½ inches (19.4 x 26.7 cm.). B.56. *Page 17*

267 March 31, 1933. 7⅝ x 10½ inches (19.4 x 26.7 cm.). B.57

268 March 31, 1933. 7⅝ x 10⁹⁄₁₆ inches (19.4 x 26.8 cm.). B.58

269 March 31, 1933. 7⅝ x 10⁹⁄₁₆ inches (19.4 x 26.8 cm.). B.59

270 March 31, 1933. 7⅝ x 10½ inches (19.4 x 26.7 cm.). B.60

271 April 3, 1933. 7⅝ x 10½ inches (19.4 x 26.7 cm.). B.64

272 April 4, 1933. 7⅝ x 10⁹⁄₁₆ inches (19.4 x 26.8 cm.). B.65

273 April 7, 1933. 14⁷⁄₁₆ x 11¹¹⁄₁₆ inches (36.7 x 29.7 cm.). B.68

274 April 8, 1933. 14½ x 11¹¹⁄₁₆ inches (36.8 x 29.7 cm.). B.69

275 April 11, 1933. 10⁹⁄₁₆ x 7⅝ inches (26.8 x 19.4 cm.). B.70

276 May 4, 1933. 10⁹⁄₁₆ x 7⅝ inches (26.8 x 19.4 cm.). B.74. *Page 14*

The Minotaur

277 May 18, 1933. 11¹¹⁄₁₆ x 14⅜ inches (29.7 x 36.6 cm.). B.85. *Page 22*

278 May 18, 1933. Etching and aquatint, 7⅝ x 10⁹⁄₁₆ inches (19.4 x 26.8 cm.). B.86. *Page 27*

279 May 23, 1933. 7⅝ x 10⁹⁄₁₆ inches (19.4 x 26.8 cm.). B.87. *Page 28*

280 May 29, 1933. 7⅝ x 10⁹⁄₁₆ inches (19.4 x 26.8 cm.). B.89. *Page 31*

The Blind Minotaur

281 September 22, 1934. Etching and engraving, 9¹⁵⁄₁₆ x 13⅝ inches (25.2 x 34.7 cm.). B.94. *Page 33*

282 *Figure.* May 1929. Lithograph, 9⅜ x 5⁹⁄₁₆ inches (23.9 x 14.2 cm.). G.246, M.XXVI. Gift of Victor S. Riesenfeld

283 *Eight Nudes.* January 13, 1946. Lithograph, 12⅝ x 17⅜ inches (32.1 x 44.2 cm.). M.29. Curt Valentin Bequest

284 *Goat.* (1952). Aquatint, printed in black, 3¹¹⁄₁₆ x 5 inches (9.3 x 12.8 cm.), for deluxe edition of André Verdet, *La Chèvre*, Paris: Editions de Beaune, 1952. The Museum of Modern Art, New York, purchase

Art Institute of Chicago: 207. Baltimore Museum of Art: 49. Anthony Bregman: 54 left. Eugene Brenwasser: 54 right. Robert Capa, LIFE Magazine © Time Inc.: jacket flap. Chevojon, Paris: 78; 101; 108; 136; 137 left. Service de Documentation Photographique, Réunion des Musées Nationaux, Versailles: 140 below; 150; 156; 176; 185; 188; 195 left, right; 197 right. Courtauld Institute: 118 left. Galerie G. Claude Bernard: 208. Galerie Louise Leiris: 160 right. John Hedgecoe: 50; 58 left; 64 below; 66; 67; 68; 69; 70; 71; 73; 74; 76; 77; 81; 82; 84; 85 below right; 86 left; 87; 88; 89; 97 above; 99; 100 left; 102; 103; 105; 106; 107; 119 below; 128; 129; 133; 158 below; 165; 174; 175; 177; 178 left; 183 below; 184; 187; 193; 194 above left, below left; 203. Bryan Heseltine: 53 above. H. Mardyks: 51 below; 55; 60; 61; 63 below right; 90; 91 right; 93; 94; 95; 97 below; 120 above left, above right; 122; 138; 139; 140 above; 142; 143 above, below left; 145 center, below; 154; 164; 169; 178 above; 190 below; 192; 196; 197 left; 198; 199; 202. O. E. Nelson: 121. Rolf Petersen: frontis. Walter Rosenblum: 159. Adolph Studly: 52; 110; 111; 112; 113 left; 114 above. Soichi Sunami: 56; 125; 126; 130; 132; 134. Tate Gallery: 83. John Webb: 51 above; 53 below; 58 right; 59; 62; 63 left, below left; 64 above; 65; 72; 75; 79; 80; 85 below left; 86 above; 91 left; 92; 96; 98; 100 right; 104; 109; 113 right; 114 left; 115; 117; 118 right; 119 above; 120 left; 123; 124; 127; 131; 135; 137 right; 141; 143 below right; 144; 145 above; 146; 147; 148; 149; 151; 152; 153; 155; 157; 158 above; 161; 162; 166; 167; 168; 170; 171; 172; 173; 179; 180; 181; 182; 183; 186; 189; 190 above; 191; 194 above right, below right; 200; 204; 205; 206.

DESIGNED BY JOSEPH BOURKE DEL VALLE. TITLE CALLIGRAPHY BY MORRIS ZASLAVSKY. TYPE SET IN LINOTYPE GRANJON BY THE COMPOSING ROOM, AND PRINTED ON MOHAWK SUPERFINE PAPER BY PHOTOGRAVURE AND COLOR COMPANY AND CRAFTON GRAPHIC COMPANY. COLOR FRONTISPIECE PRINTED BY LEBANON VALLEY OFFSET COMPANY. BOUND BY J. F. TAPLEY COMPANY. FIRST EDITION, SEPTEMBER, 1967, 78,000 COPIES.